The German, Flemish and Dutch Drawings

Great Drawings
of the Louvre Museum

The German, Flemish and Dutch Drawings

Roseline Bacou, *Curator at the Cabinet des Dessins*

with the collaboration of Arlette Calvet

George Braziller *New York*

Translated from the French by Marguerite Hugo

Published in 1968.
All rights reserved.
No part of the contents of this book
may be reproduced without the written consent of the publisher,
George Braziller, Inc.
One Park Avenue, New York, N.Y. 10016.

Library of Congress Catalog Card Number 68-23040.

Printed in Holland by Joh. Enschedé en Zonen, Haarlem

Table of Contents

The beauty and mastery of a great drawing impress us immediately. No special knowledge of Dürer or his period is needed to respond to the miracle of aptness and suggestive poetry effected, for example, in the *View of Arco*. If we are to deepen and sustain our appreciation, however, we must seek beyond our first impression. Behind a few simple lines or touches of color lies an adventure, open to everyone. The observer can attempt, from these brief indications, to rediscover the unique moment of creation, to discern the artist's intentions, and finally, to know the artist himself, whose drawing is a personal revelation.

For the artist, a drawing represents a simple sketch of a given subject, a stage in his research, or, in some cases, a definitive work. The attentive "amateur" considers each drawing an end in itself, containing and revealing, despite its fragility and its small dimensions, the entire personality of the artist.

In this respect, nothing is more significant than the technique used in the creation of a drawing. The means of expression favored by a master reveals not only the nature of his artistic quest, but also his most profound aspirations. His choice of a medium may be conditioned to some extent by contemporary taste; the widespread use of brown wash in the xvii century, the development of the "trois crayons" in the xviii, the preference for watercolor in the following century, indicate the artistic tendencies common to a given period. However, the creative genius imposes his own style and selects the means of expression best suited to his interpretation of a subject and personal approach to his work; thus, at the end of the xv century, when the "carta tinta," involving the use of metalpoint on prepared paper, was especially favored by Florentine artists, Leonardo da Vinci initiated the use of red chalk, and Signorelli experimented in his nude studies with the possibilities offered by black chalk.

Certain artists have confined themselves almost exclusively to one technique, learning to exploit the secrets and powers of a single language. Use of pen and ink heightened with wash enabled Rembrandt to express the dramatic intensity of the Passion of Christ, to project the personality of a model, or to capture the ephemeral ray of light playing over a landscape. Other artists exercise extraordinary freedom in their choice. Rubens, for example, mastered a wide range of techniques; his genius lay in his ability to adapt them to different subjects and circumstances, while satisfying the demands of his inspiration.

More than any other art form, drawing brings out the fundamental difference between two types of artists: those who spontaneously translate their immediate impressions of reality into black and white, and those who express themselves in color. An artist fascinated by the interplay of lines and sharp contrasts of light and shadow will employ pen and ink, black chalk, and heavy washes, while the artist who sees the world in terms of color will prefer red chalk, pastels, or the highlights of watercolor. But whatever the means of expression, a drawing always reflects the profound nature of its creator; employed by a colorist like Rubens, even black chalk seems to take on a kind of coloration.

The earliest drawings presented here from the German, Flemish and Dutch schools are all executed in metalpoint. Yet, when the Flemish painter, Van der Weyden, working on paper prepared with bone powder, delineates the face of the Virgin, the spiritualized quality of the single pure line contrasts with the precision and realism of portraits by Holbein the Elder, a German painter using the same technique. Unlike the Florentines, who chose prepared paper in bright, luminous colors—blues, pinks, mauves—Northern artists preferred more muted tones, like pearl gray and ivory beige, at the end of the xv century, or toward the beginning of the xvi, dark green and brown. A remarkable example of the freedom achieved by a master of the difficult art of metalpoint, which demands absolute sureness of hand and allows no going back, is found in the sketchbook attributed to Gerard David, where each line, far from being mere virtuoso performance, reveals the emotion of the artist.

In the significant choice of technique, the engraver inclines toward pen and ink, which can reproduce the tight linear construction and cross-hatching obtained with a burin; drawings in this technique by Master E.S., Dürer, or his pupil, Baldung Grien, testify to their training and skill in the art of engraving. For Bosch, the pen is the tool of minute analysis, serving to delineate, with singular credibility, the fantastic and monstrous creatures born of his imagination. It enabled Brueghel, in the Alps, and Roeland Savery, in the Tyrol, to create vast panoramic landscapes, so infinitely detailed they make the head spin. And during the Mannerist period, it is employed with captivating virtuosity as a vehicle for the boldly felicitous achievements of Spranger, the graceful arabesques which define the sinuous female forms evoked by Goltzius, and the suggestive figures created by Jacob de Gheyn. Often pen and ink are heightened with wash, which gives depth and contrast and sometimes, as in Holbein the Younger's sketches for decorative compositions or Van Orley's projects for tapestries, a pictorial effect anticipating the final work. Both Rembrandt and Rubens work with brown wash on white paper, yet the results are as different as the nature of their genius; Rubens displays verve and dynamism, while Rembrandt's smallest sketch shows concentration and depth of feeling.

A pioneer in the use of black chalk, Dürer employed it in portraits with a breadth and rigor of treatment which render both the physical aspect of the model and his personality. The *Portrait of Erasmus*, for example, is a remarkable demonstration of his masterly draughtsmanship and intelligent exploitation of the resources of a particular technique. When Lucas van Leyden, who wished to equal the German master's achievements in the art of portraiture, introduced black chalk into Holland, he created a tradition to which Dutch and Flemish portraitists remained faithful. Using red and white chalk to heighten the black, Rubens generously suffuses with vitality the full-blown beauty of his female nudes, the smooth texture of a cheek, or the brightness of a gaze. For the best portraitists of the Rembrandt school—Jan Lievens or the austere Cornelis Visscher—shadings of black chalk suffice; the simplicity of expression achieved through this technique gives added force to their exceptional psychological insight. In the landscapes of Van Goyen we find a similar economy of means serving a refined sensibility; black chalk and China ink wash recapture the gray harmonies of dusk, reflections on calm waters, horizons shrouded in fog. Of a more dramatic temperament, Ruysdael uses black chalk to sharpen contrasts; in views of windswept dunes, light and shadow are cast by a menacing sky over vast, melancholy landscapes.

While certain artists are thus experimenting with black and white, the Northern love of color begins to assert itself in drawing. In the impressive *Portrait of Margarethe Prellwitz*, a masterpiece of early xv century drawing in Germany, Grünewald abandons his usual technique of slightly blurred black chalk for extremely forceful touches of color, which intensify the expressionism of the pain-distorted face. In the field of watercolor Dürer is again an innovator, creating landscapes of unprecedented freedom, at once highly organized and lyrical, realistic and strongly subjective. When compared to works so modern in concept, the meticulous execution and unreal coloration of the gouache landscapes drawn by Hans Bol in the xvi century, as settings for Biblical or contemporary scenes, seem bound by the conventions of the miniature tradition. Light touches of watercolor also heighten the drawings of certain Mannerists and the landscapes of Paul Bril, in which colored notations subtly play over the solid structure in brown wash.

The xvii century marks the triumph of color in Flemish drawings. With supreme ease Rubens dashes off brilliant sketches in watercolor or oil paint on paper. Gouache is used by Fouquières in boldly conceived landscapes which anticipate the innovations of xix century artists, and Jordaens creates a series of watercolors remarkable for their breadth and savory treatment. Even the colored notations—discreet and amazingly apt—made by Van der Meulen in his battlefield sketches reveal the feeling for color which is inherent in the Flemish genius. The influence of these works, amplified by the actual presence in Paris of many Flemish painters, proved determinant in the orientation of French painting toward richer and more highly colored forms, at the end of the century.

Following Rembrandt's example, most Dutch artists chose pen and brown ink for their religious and historical drawings. But for popular subjects like the landscape, the genre scene, or the still life they frequently turned to watercolor. Within a narrow range of extremely sober tones, Lambert Doomer, for example, creates highly personal and intense drawings, while Eeckhout colors some of his landscapes with harmonious half-tints which reflect a particularly refined sensibility. Village scenes conceived like small paintings by Van Ostade were at one time very much admired. Modern taste, it is true, tends to prefer the rapid calligraphy of his pen and ink sketches to these highly finished and somewhat conventionally colored works. On the other hand, the elaborate watercolor studies executed by Van Huysum for his paintings of flowers are as prized by connoisseurs today as they were by the greatest "amateurs" of the XVIII century.

The selection of drawings reproduced in this volume illustrates the great diversity of techniques used in drawing. It also attests to the high quality of the works by German, Flemish and Dutch masters found in the portfolios of the Cabinet des Dessins. We owe most of the information in the accompanying legends to the outstanding research of Louis Demonts and Frits Lugt, who compiled the series of inventories of works representing the Northern schools in the Louvre. To them we wish to extend our gratitude on this occasion.

ROSELINE BACOU

Index of Artists

Works Cited in an Abbreviated Form

DEMONTS, 1937-1938

MUSÉE DU LOUVRE. INVENTAIRE GÉNÉRAL DES DESSINS DES ECOLES DU NORD. ECOLES ALLEMANDE ET SUISSE, by Louis Demonts, Paris, vol. I, 1937; vol. II, 1938.

LUGT

F. Lugt, LES MARQUES DE COLLECTIONS DE DESSINS ET D'ESTAMPES, Amsterdam, 1921; Supplément, The Hague, 1956.

LUGT, *Flamands*, 1949

MUSÉE DU LOUVRE. INVENTAIRE GÉNÉRAL DES DESSINS DES ECOLES DU NORD. ECOLE FLAMANDE, by Frits Lugt, Paris, 1949, 2 vols.

LUGT, *Hollandais* 1929-1931-1933

MUSÉE DU LOUVRE. INVENTAIRE GÉNÉRAL DES DESSINS DES ECOLES DU NORD. ECOLE HOLLANDAISE, by Frits Lugt, Paris, vol. I, 1929; vol. II, 1931; vol. III, 1933.

TIETZE and TIETZE-CONRAT, 1928

H. Tietze and E. Tietze-Conrat, DER JUNGE DÜRER. VERZEICHNIS DER WERKE BIS ZUR VENEZIANISCHEN REISE IM JAHRE 1505, Augsbourg, 1928.

TIETZE and TIETZE-CONRAT, 1937

H. Tietze and E. Tietze-Conrat, KRITISCHES VERZEICHNIS DER WERKE ALBRECHT DÜRERS, Band II, DER REISE DÜRER. ERSTER HALBAND VON DER VENEZIANISCHEN REISE IM JAHRE 1505 BIS ZUR NIEDERLANDISCHEN REISE IM JAHRE 1520 NEBST NACHTRÄGEN AUS DEN JAHREN 1492-1505, Basel-Leipzig, 1937.

TIETZE and TIETZE-CONRAT, 1938

H. Tietze and E. Tietze-Conrat, KRITISCHES VERZEICHNIS DER WERKE ALBRECHT DÜRERS, Band II, ZWEITER HALBAND. VON DER NIEDERLÄNDISCHEN REISE IM JAHRE 1520 BIS ZUM TODE DES MEISTERS 1528, Basel-Leipzig, 1938.

The Drawings

Master E.S.
1467

1. *The Baptism of Christ*

TECHNIQUE. Pen and black ink. (29.5 x 21.5 cm.).

PROVENANCE. Acquired by the Louvre during the Revolution.
Inventory 18.838.

BIBLIOGRAPHY. M. Lehrs, "Über einige Zeichnungen des Meisters E. S.," in *Jahrbuch der Königlich Preussischen Kunstsammlungen*, XI, 1890, pp. 79-84, repr. opp. p. 82.
M. Geisberg, *Der Meister E. S.*, Leipzig, 1924, pl. 66.
Demonts, 1937, no. 265, vol. I, pl. XCII.
Master E. S. Five Hundredth Anniversary Exhibition, Exhibition Catalogue, Philadelphia Museum of Art, 1967, no. 83, repr.

An important exhibition of works by Master E. S., known only by the monogram on eighteen of his engravings, was recently held in Philadelphia. This prolific and complex engraver was one of the leading figures in German graphic art at the end of the XV century, before Martin Schongauer. He appears to have worked mainly in the region of the Upper Rhine, where he was influenced by contemporary Flemish painting as well as by sculpture. He in turn was to exert an unmistakable influence on the local engravers, goldsmiths, and stained glass artists, who copied his particular style of drapery with abundant, broken folds and his angular figures, shown in distorted attitudes.

The *Baptism of Christ* and *Saint Catherine*, in the Berlin Museum, are the only drawings unanimously attributed to Master E. S. In the Louvre drawing, considered one of his most beautiful early creations, the fine crosshatching used to describe the modeling and shading corresponds to the cuts in some of his first engravings, executed around 1445, *Augustus and the Sibyl*, for example, or the *Man of Sorrows*. Two later engravings repeat the same scene, but with an abundance of detail which contrasts with the balance and simplicity of the present composition. According to L. Fischel, the latter may derive from a painting by the Master of 1445, which has since disappeared.   A.C.

Hans Holbein the Elder

About 1465 - 1529

2. *Portrait of Ulrich Schwartz*

TECHNIQUE. Silverpoint on prepared paper. (12.6 x 9.9 cm.). Inscribed in pen and ink at upper center: *ALT. ULRICH SCHVVRCZZ* (the last word has been written over to read *SCHVVARCZ*); below, near the left edge of sheet: *H.*

PROVENANCE. Acquired by the Louvre during the Revolution. Inventory 18.898.

BIBLIOGRAPHY. A. Woltman, *Holbein und seine Zeit, Des Künstlers Familie, Leben und Schaffen*, Leipzig, II, 1876, p. 87, no. 268.
C. Glaser, *Hans Holbein der Ältere*, Leipzig, 1908, p. 200, no. 147.
Demonts, 1937, vol. I, no. 213, pl. LXXII.
N. Lieb and A. Stange, *Hans Holbein der Ältere*, 1960, no. 284, fig. 364.

Recent studies have identified the figure shown here as Ulrich Schwartz the Younger (1448/49–1519) and not his father, Ulrich the Elder, Burgomaster of Augsburg, as the inscription seemed to indicate. The drawing is believed to have served for a composition by Narziss Renner, conceived in 1522 and called the *Geschlechtertanz (Dance of the Generations)*. Renner's work is known through the badly damaged original now in the Maximilian Museum in Augsburg, and a copy, better preserved, in Berlin (repr. G. Habich, "Der Augsburger Geschlechtertanz von 1522," in *Jahrbuch der Königlich preussischen Kunstsammlungen*, 1911, between pp. 214–215). The present work can also be related to the *Votive Portrait of the Schwartz Family*, painted by Holbein the Elder in 1508 (repr. *Die Malerfamilie Holbein*, Exhibition Catalogue, Basel, 1960, pl. 2).
The rounded, realistic treatment of the *Portrait of Ulrich Schwartz* may be compared to that of the portraits of monks in the Monastery of Saint Afra and Saint Ulrich in Augsburg, drawn at approximately the same period. At this time, the artist's graphic language acquired a suppleness and subtlety in the description of volumes which were to influence the early works of Holbein the Younger.   A.C.

3. *Portrait of a Woman*

TECHNIQUE. Metalpoint, heightened with red chalk and white, on prepared paper. (13.9 x 10 cm.). Inscribed in pen and ink at upper center: *brustbild* (?).

PROVENANCE. His de la Salle; stamp at lower center (Lugt 1333); given to the Louvre in 1878.
Inventory RF 738.

BIBLIOGRAPHY. C. Glaser, *Hans Holbein der Ältere*, Leipzig, 1908, p. 206, no. 212.
Demonts, 1937, vol. I, no. 215, pl. LXXII.
N. Lieb and A. Stange, *Hans Holbein der Ältere*, 1960, no. 292, fig. 369.

Here, a sharp, precise delineation stripped of all ornamental effect reveals to what extent the work of Holbein the Elder, especially the metalpoint portraits, follows the tradition of the Flemish masters of the Van Eyck school (see no. 34).
In the Copenhagen Museum there is another *Portrait of a Young Woman*, in which the figure—probably the same model—is shown to the waist and turned toward the right (repr. N. Lieb and A. Stange, fig. 368). The present study can also be related to the *Portrait of a Young Girl* in the Ecole des Beaux-Arts in Paris (repr. *idem*, fig. 313). Recent studies (*Die Malerfamilie Holbein*, Exhibition Catalogue, Basel, 1960) tend to date these drawings around 1515–1516, a period when the transition from Gothic art to that of the Renaissance is apparent in the work of Holbein the Elder.   A.C.

ALT·VLRICH·SCHVVARCZ·

Albrecht Dürer

1471 - 1528

4. *View of Arco*

TECHNIQUE. Watercolor, heightened with gouache, partly reworked by the artist in pen and black ink. (22.3 x 22.2 cm.). Inscribed in pen and ink at upper right: *fenedier klawsen*, with monogram.

PROVENANCE. E. Jabach; paraphs on verso (Lugt 2959 and 2953) and the number: *cinq*. Purchased for the Royal Collection in 1671. Inventory 18.579.

BIBLIOGRAPHY. Tietze and Tietze-Conrat, 1928, p. 24, no. 92, pl. 92, pp. 315–316.
F. Winkler, *Die Zeichnungen Albrecht Dürers*, Berlin, I, 1936, no. 94, pl. 94.
Demonts, 1937, vol. I, no. 144, pl. LVII.
E. Panofsky, *The Life and Art of Albrecht Dürer*, Princeton, New Jersey, 1948, II, no. 1378.

Shortly after his marriage to Agnes Frey, Dürer visited Italy for the first time. During the trip he executed some fifteen watercolor landscapes, some of which are now in Vienna, Berlin, Bremen, and London. The Louvre watercolor—one of the most famous in the series—was probably drawn upon his return from Venice, in the spring of 1495. According to K. Gerstenberg, the site is the fortress of Arco in the Tyrol, on the border of the Venetian Republic; more recently, however, Mrs. Ellingham has rather convincingly suggested that it may be the citadel of San Marino.

When one considers that at this time painters had scarcely begun to introduce studies after nature into their paintings, Dürer's achievements in landscape representation seem quite remarkable. In the present drawing, he reconstructs the topography of the scene in a precise, descriptive style which recalls his views of the country around Nuremberg, executed shortly before his trip to Italy; at the same time, he attempts, with subtle analysis, to render the luminous poetry and color values of the spring landscape. This progressive conquest of atmosphere in landscape, which is one of the preoccupations of the Renaissance, distinguishes Dürer as an artist already touched by the modernist inspiration of the XVI century.   A.C.

Albrecht Dürer

1471 - 1528

5. *Madonna and Child*

The Virgin is surrounded by Saint Joseph, Saint Anne, Saint Joachim and the young Saint John the Baptist.

TECHNIQUE. Pen and black ink (for most of the composition), pen and brown ink (figure of Saint Anne, hatched passages in the sky, feet of Saint Joachim, stones in foreground). (28.1 x 21.3 cm.). Dated in pen and ink at lower center: *1519*, with monogram below. Numbered in pen and ink at lower right: *24*.

PROVENANCE. P. J. Mariette; stamp at lower left (Lugt 1852); sale, Paris, 1775, no. 889. Bought at this sale for the Royal Collection. Inventory 18.582.

BIBLIOGRAPHY. Tietze and Tietze-Conrat, 1937, no. 738, repr. p. 299.
Demonts, 1937, vol. I, no. 102, pl. XXXVI.
F. Winkler, *Die Zeichnungen Albrecht Dürers*, Berlin, III, 1938, no. 535, repr.
E. Panofsky, *The Life and Art of Albrecht Dürer*, Princeton, New Jersey, 1948, II, no. 731.

The cult of the Virgin, which was extremely popular in Nuremberg until the Reformation, was to find in Dürer one of its most ardent illustrators. Of all the themes related to the life of the Virgin, one of the most important in the drawings he executed around 1510–1520 was that of the Virgin and Child. As in the present, highly representative work, this subject is the occasion for intimately tender scenes, filled with serenity.

Though not directly related to a painted or engraved work (there is, however, some connection with two wood engravings, one dated 1518, from the series representing the *Life of the Virgin*, and another dated 1526), the drawing reproduced is part of a series of studies through which Dürer evolved from a traditional representation of Mary and the Christ Child (Winkler, no. 512) to that of the Madonna and Child with saints (see no. 12, in particular). The curved delineation, the concision and classic grouping make this *Holy Family* one of the most beautiful drawings by Dürer in Mariette's collection. While remaining true to nature, his art has undergone the refining influence of direct contact with Italy, thus achieving exceptional formal beauty.   A.C.

Albrecht Dürer

1471 – 1528

6. *Three Studies of a Helmet*

TECHNIQUE. Brush, pen and indigo for the metal of the helmet, heightened with white; brown or green wash for the lacings, straps and nails, reworked by the artist in pen and black ink; traces of pen and brown ink under helmet at upper left. (42.1 x 26.7 cm.). Dated in pen and brown ink at upper center: *1514*, with monogram; at lower left, traces of the monogram in blue ink.

PROVENANCE. Baummeville. L. Bonnat; stamp at lower right (Lugt 1714); given to the Louvre in 1923.
Inventory RF 5640.

BIBLIOGRAPHY. Tietze and Tietze-Conrat, 1928, no. 210, repr. p. 193, fig. 210.
F. Winkler, *Die Zeichnungen Albrecht Dürers*, Berlin, I, 1936, no. 177, pl. 177.
Demonts, 1937, vol. I, no. 146, pl. LIX.
E. Panofsky, *The Life and Art of Albrecht Dürer*, Princeton, New Jersey, 1948, II, no. 1447.

While reminiscent of Dürer's apprenticeship in the workshop of his goldsmith father, these studies also show the artist as a subtle colorist. In fact, this sheet, a tour de force of detailed precision from the technical point of view, is saved from the dry and purely documentary by its fresh and finely shaded tones. The date marked on the drawing is no doubt apocryphal, and Dürer scholars generally agree, on the strength of comparison with his other drawings from the same period, notably the *Armored Horseman* in the same technique, now in the Albertina (repr. Winkler, I, fig. 176), that this work was executed around 1498. According to A. M. Cetto (*Aquarelles d' Albrecht Dürer*, Basel, 1954, pp. 7, 17) the helmet used as a model was probably similar to the one in the Higgins Armoury Museum in Worcester, but from an earlier period. In any case, the helmet represented in profile at upper left reappears in a copper engraving entitled *Armorial Bearings with Death's Head* (J. Meder, *Ein Handbuch über Albrecht Dürers Stiche...*, 1932, no. 98); the helmet represented frontally reappears, with a few variations, in the copper engraving of *Armorial Bearings with a Helmet* (Meder, *idem*, no. 97), which was executed around 1503.   A.C.

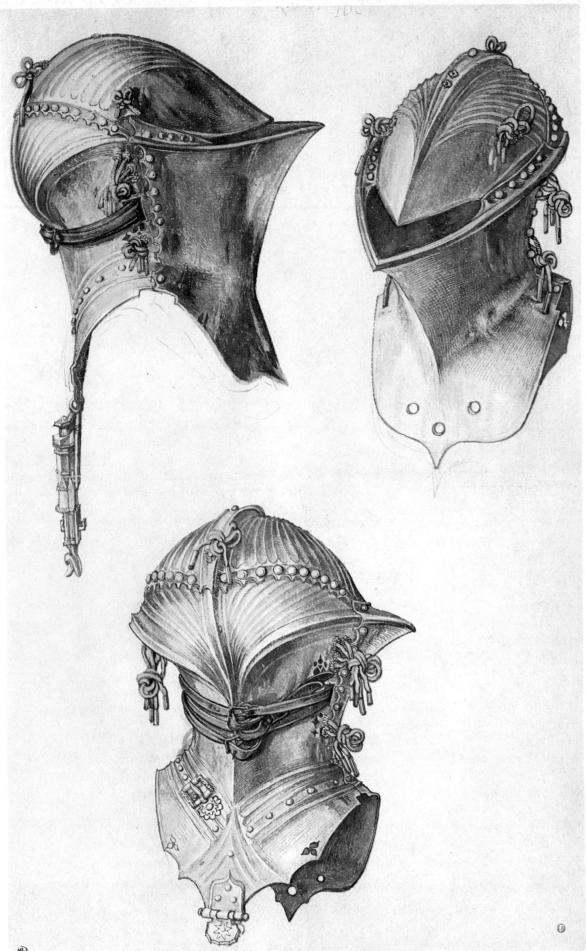

Albrecht Dürer

1471 - 1528

7. Head of a Child

TECHNIQUE. Pen and ink, brush and gray ink, heightened with white, on blue paper. (12.9 x 10.1 cm.). Inscribed in pen and brown ink at lower left: *Albert durer F.*

PROVENANCE. The Royal Collection; paraph of Antoine Coypel (Lugt 478). Inventory 18.602.

BIBLIOGRAPHY. Demonts, 1937, vol. I, no. 133, pl. LIII.
Tietze and Tietze-Conrat, 1937, p. 24, no. 299, repr. p. 179, fig. 299.
F. Winkler, *Die Zeichnungen Albrecht Dürers*, Berlin, II, 1937, no. 397, fig. 397.
E. Panofsky, *The Life and Art of Albrecht Dürer*, Princeton, New Jersey, 1948, I, p. 111; II, p. 81, no. 755, p. 171.

8. Head of a Child

TECHNIQUE. Pen and ink, brush and gray ink, heightened with white, on blue paper. (12.7 x 9.4 cm.). Inscribed in pen and brown ink at lower left: *d' Albert Dürer.*

PROVENANCE. The Royal Collection. Inventory 18.608.

BIBLIOGRAPHY. Demonts, 1937, vol. I, no. 135, pl. LIII.
Tietze and Tietze-Conrat, 1937, p. 24, no. 300; repr. p. 179, fig. 300.
F. Winkler, *Die Zeichnungen Albrecht Dürers*, Berlin, II, 1937, no. 398, fig. 398.
E. Panofsky, *The Life and Art of Albrecht Dürer*, Princeton, New Jersey, 1948, I, p. 111; II, p. 81, no. 755, p. 171.

It is likely that this study of a child's head, probably dating from the time of Dürer's second trip to Italy (1505–1507), was originally intended for a painting entitled the *Madonna of the Rose Garlands* (1506, Prague Museum), which was commissioned for the chapel of the Fondaco dei Tedeschi. A number of preparatory studies of "putti" and angels for this painting are known; however, neither the present drawing nor the following one appears in the final composition. They are seen instead at upper left in the Heller triptych, which was completed in 1509. The second of the two heads may even be related to the angel near the young Saint John the Baptist in the *Madonna with the Canary*, dated 1506 and now in Berlin (E. Flechsig, *Albrecht Dürer, sein Leben und seine künstlerische Entwicklung*, Berlin, II, 1931, pp. 336–337). The Louvre claims at least six more such studies of children's heads, connected with both the *Madonna of the Rose Garlands* and the Heller triptych.

Comparison of the sure graphic skill displayed by the artist in these works—reminiscent in style of Giovanni Bellini, whom Dürer met in 1505—with the draughtsmanship of the *Christ Child*, executed after Lorenzo di Credi (Louvre, Inventory RF 4662) eleven years earlier, clearly illustrates how much Dürer had gained from direct contact with Italian art.   A.C.

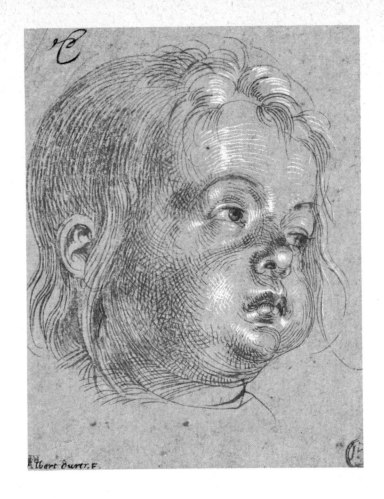

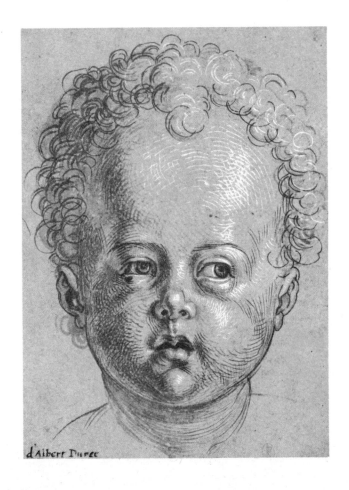

Albrecht Dürer
1471 – 1528

9. *Study of a Drapery*

TECHNIQUE. Brush and black ink, heightened with white, on green prepared paper. (25.5 x 19 cm.). Dated at lower center with brush: *1508*, and signed with monogram.

PROVENANCE. Baron Vivant-Denon; stamp at lower right (Lugt 779); sale, Paris, 1826, no. 625. Baron de Silvestre; sale, Paris, 1851, no. 148. Purchased by the Louvre in 1852.
Inventory 18.597.

BIBLIOGRAPHY. Ch. Ephrussi, *Etude sur le triptyque d'Albert Dürer, dit le tableau d'autel d'Heller*, Paris, 1876, p. 16, repr. between pp. 22 and 23.
Demonts, 1937, vol. I, no. 116, pl. XLIV.
E. Winkler, *Die Zeichnungen Albrecht Dürers*, Berlin, II, 1937, no. 455, pl. 455.
Tietze and Tietze-Conrat, 1937, p. 44, no. 367, repr. p. 195, fig. 367.
E. Panofsky, *The Life and Art of Albrecht Dürer*, Princeton, New Jersey, 1948, I, p. 123; II, no. 499.

This is a study for Christ's Coronation of the Virgin, at upper left of the central panel of the triptych which was commissioned by Jacob Heller around 1503 and placed in the Saint Thomas Chapel of the Dominican church in Frankfort in 1509 (repr. Ephrussi, opp. pp. 1, 3, and 5). This central panel, the only one executed entirely by Dürer, was sold to Maximilian I, Elector of Bavaria, in 1615. It was later burned in the fire which destroyed the Palace of Munich in 1759; but a copy, made by Jobst Harrich at the time of the purchase of the original, still exists in Frankfort, with the right wing-panel, which is all that remains of the original triptych. More than twenty related drawings are known, all of them brush studies executed on prepared paper. In addition to the present sheet, there are seven studies of children's heads in the Louvre; the other studies are in the Albertina, Berlin, and Bremen Museums.

In an exhibition of XVI century European art in the Louvre (1965), comparison of Dürer's drapery study with an equally famous one by Leonardo da Vinci (Inventory 2255), executed ten years earlier, brought out the differences underlying the concepts of the two artists. Leonardo's simple, monumental study has a universal quality. Dürer's drawing is no less remarkable for its breadth; yet his treatment of the twisted and slightly stiff folds is still bound by the example of German Gothic sculpture.   A.C.

Albrecht Dürer

1471 - 1528

10. *Portrait of Erasmus*

TECHNIQUE. Black chalk. (37.1 x 26.7 cm.). Dated at upper part, towards the right: *1520*. Inscribed below: *Erasmus fon rottertam*.

PROVENANCE. S. van Huls; sale, The Hague, 1736. General Count Andreossy; sale, Paris, 1864, no. 61. J. Gigoux; sale, Paris, 1882, no. 288. L. Bonnat; stamp at lower right (Lugt 1714); given to the Louvre in 1912. Inventory RF 4113.

BIBLIOGRAPHY. Demonts, 1937, vol. I, no. 127, pl. XLIX.
Tietze and Tietze-Conrat, 1938, p. 12, no. 760, repr. p. 153, fig. 760.
F. Winkler, *Die Zeichnungen Albrecht Dürers*, Berlin, IV, 1939, no. 805, pl. 805.
E. Panofsky, *The Life and Art of Albrecht Dürer*, Princeton, New Jersey, 1948, I, pp. 214, 239; II, no. 1020.
Albert Dürer. Lettres et écrits théoriques. Traité des proportions. Text translated and presented by Pierre Vaisse, Paris, 1964, p. 125.

It is probable that this second portrait of the famous humanist, drawn by Dürer during his trip to the Netherlands (July 12, 1520–July 1521), was used for the copperplate engraving he executed eleven years later (Bartsch, 107). His *Travel Journal* indicates that he met with Erasmus at least four times during the trip, principally in Antwerp, between August 5 and 19, 1520, and again in Brussels, between August 26 and September 3 of the same year (A. Gerlo, *Erasme et ses portraitistes*, Brussels, 1950, pp. 25–26).

Dürer's first portrait, probably dating from the meeting in Antwerp when the artist received several gifts from Erasmus, has disappeared. The fact that he executed the present drawing is confirmed by a statement in the *Travel Journal*: "I have made a new portrait of Erasmus of Rotterdam," and by several references to the same portrait in letters from Erasmus to Willibald Pirckheimer. This work, which was begun in Brussels, appears to have been left unfinished. As E. Panofsky has noted, the black chalk background generally utilized by Dürer to make the faces of his models stand out has not been filled in. It is nonetheless a swiftly and powerfully executed drawing, which ranks, with the portraits painted by Holbein shortly after, as one of the most important elements in the iconography of Erasmus.   A.C.

Erasmus von Rotterdam

Albrecht Dürer
1471 - 1528

11. *Portrait of a Young Man Shown to the Waist*

TECHNIQUE. Black chalk on watermarked paper. (41.2 x 27.7 cm.). Dated at
upper part: *1520*, with monogram.

PROVENANCE. General Count Andreossy. Th. Lawrence. Ch. S. Bale; stamp on
verso (Lugt 646); sale, London, 1881, no. 2283. Thibaudeau. L. Bonnat; stamp
at lower center (Lugt 1714); given to the Louvre in 1923.
Inventory RF 5639.

BIBLIOGRAPHY. Demonts, 1937, vol. I, no. 128, pl. V.
Tietze and Tietze-Conrat, 1938, no. 759, pl. 759.
F. Winkler, *Die Zeichnungen Albrecht Dürers*, Berlin, IV, 1939, no. 806, pl. 806
and detail pl. 806a.
E. Panofsky, *The Life and Art of Albrecht Dürer*, Princeton, New Jersey, 1948,
II, no. 1070.

Like the *Portrait of Erasmus* (see no. 10), this forceful drawing dates
from the time of Dürer's visit to the Netherlands. It is representative of the evolution in his painted and drawn portraits of this
period; he continues, in the medieval tradition, to give an exact
rendition of the outward appearance of his models, while attempt-
ing, through a broadening of his vision, to express their inner
reality. This aspiration, corresponding to the Renaissance glorifi-
cation of the individual, is felt most strongly in Dürer's black
chalk portraits, executed from 1514 on (*Portrait of His Mother*,
1514, Albertina; *Portrait of a Young Man*, 1520, Berlin). In the
present study, the particularly sober and free treatment in black
chalk gives the unknown figure an intensity of expression rarely
attained.

This new conception of the portrait was brought to the Netherlands by Dürer himself, where it strongly influenced some of his
contemporaries, notably Lucas van Leyden. The latter, whom
Dürer met in Antwerp around May of 1521 and of whom he made
a drawn portrait (Rennes), was the first of the Dutch artists to
employ black chalk, using it in his portraits with a virtuosity and
a power of observation comparable to Dürer's (see nos. 69–70).

A.C.

Albrecht Dürer
1471 - 1528

12. *The Virgin and Child among Saints*

The names of the figures on either side of the Virgin's throne are inscribed above their heads: Jacob, Joseph, Joachim, Zachary, David, Elisabeth, Anne.

TECHNIQUE. Pen and brown ink on watermarked paper. (31 x 44.5 cm.).

PROVENANCE. Baron Vivant-Denon; stamp at lower right (Lugt 779); sale, Paris, 1826, no. 603. J. E. Gatteaux; stamp at lower right (Lugt 851); bequest to the Louvre in 1881.
Inventory RF 1079.

BIBLIOGRAPHY. E. Heidrich, *Geschichte des Dürerschen Marienbildes*, Leipzig, 1906, pp. 144, 206-209, fig. 21.
Demonts, 1937, vol. I, no. 104, pl. XXXVII.
Tietze and Tietze-Conrat, 1938, p. 31, no. 847, repr. p. 172, fig. 847.
F. Winkler, *Die Zeichnungen Albrecht Dürers*, Berlin, IV, 1939, no. 838, pl. 838.
E. Panofsky, *The Life and Art of Albrecht Dürer*, Princeton, New Jersey, 1948, I, pp. 227-228; II, no. 762, fig. 285.

Several drawings on the same subject, notably in Chantilly and Bayonne, have been related to this composition, a project for a painting which Dürer is believed to have conceived after his return from the Netherlands, toward the middle of 1521. The painting was apparently never executed, and no document establishing its purpose has been found; however, in view of the number and quality of the preparatory drawings, it seems likely that the artist envisaged a major work, comparable to the Heller triptych. In addition to fifteen composition sketches—horizontal and vertical—which represent the Virgin and Child amidst a number of figures ranging from five to fifteen, there are several studies, some of them highly elaborated, for isolated figures (see no. 13), draperies, and a chorus of angels.

Like the Bayonne sketch, the present study is planned in the manner of a Venetian *Sacra Conversazione*. At the same time, the theme of the Holy Infancy is introduced, showing the influence of Memling or Metsys, whose works the artist had occasion to see in the Netherlands. This skillful synthesis of two different concepts of beauty is one of the most brilliant testimonials to the genius of Dürer.   A.C.

Albrecht Dürer

1471 - 1528

13. *Portrait of a Young Girl Shown to the Waist*

TECHNIQUE. Black chalk, heightened with white, on green prepared paper. (41.5 x 28.6 cm.). Dated at upper right: *1521*, with monogram below.

PROVENANCE. E. Jabach; paraph at lower left (Lugt 2961). Purchased for the Royal Collection in 1671.
Inventory 18.590.

BIBLIOGRAPHY. E. Heidrich, *Geschichte des Dürerschen Marienbildes*, Leipzig, 1906, pp. 207, 208.
Demonts, 1937, vol. I, no. 129, pl. LI.
Tietze and Tietze-Conrat, 1938, p. 33, no. 852, repr. p. 173, fig. 852.
F. Winkler, *Die Zeichnungen Albrecht Dürers*, Berlin, IV, 1939, no. 845, pl. 845.
E. Panofsky, *The Life and Art of Albrecht Dürer*, Princeton, New Jersey, 1948, I, pp. 204, 288; II, no. 769, fig. 289.

Since the publication of Wöllflin's book in 1905, this large study has been classified among various drawings related to a painting of the Virgin which Dürer had planned to paint after his return from the Netherlands, but, in fact, never executed. The half-length figure of a young girl is that of Saint Barbara whose silhouette is seen at left of the Virgin's throne in the pen and ink composition sketch now in the Louvre (see no. 12) and in two sketches in the Bayonne Museum.

The broad supple style of the present drawing contrasts with the rapid, elliptic treatment of the more complete studies, but is found in other drawings of isolated figures related to the same painting, notably the enigmatic *Saint Apollonia* in the Berlin Museum (Winkler, no. 846), also dated 1521, or the head of Saint Joseph, in the British Museum (Winkler, no. 848). Another Louvre study in the same technique represents the profile of Saint Catherine and the clasped hands of Saint Joachim (Inventory RF 1080). The sense of the monumental displayed in the latter drawing is evidence of the mastery which the artist had attained at the height of his maturity.   A.C.

Albrecht Dürer

1471 - 1528

14. *The Virgin and Two Holy Women*

TECHNIQUE. Black chalk, heightened with white, on green prepared paper. (42 x 30.7 cm.). Dated at upper center: *1521*, with monogram below.

PROVENANCE. General Count Andreossy. Th. Lawrence; stamp at lower left (Lugt 2445). H. Defer Dumesnil; stamp at lower left (Lugt 739); sale, Paris, 1900, no. 35, repr. Dr. Tuffier. In trust with the Louvre.

BIBLIOGRAPHY. Demonts, 1937, vol. I, cited under no. 13.
Tietze and Tietze-Conrat, 1938, p. 33, no. 852, repr. p. 173, fig. 852.
F. Winkler, *Die Zeichnungen Albrecht Dürers*, Berlin, IV, 1939, no. 858, pl. 858.
E. Panofsky, *The Life and Art of Albrecht Dürer*, Princeton, New Jersey, 1948, I, pp. 204, 224; II, no. 535, fig. 284.

The present drawing, treated with the monumental simplicity characteristic of Dürer's late works, is a preparatory study for the group of Holy Women at the foot of the Cross in an unfinished engraving known as the *Great Crucifixion*, datable 1523 (J. Meder, *Dürer-Katalog, Ein Handbuch über Albrecht Dürers Stiche. Radierungen, Holzschnitte, derenzustande Ausgaben und Wasser-zeichen*, Vienna, 1932, no. 25). The authenticity of the engraving, early prints of which are extremely rare, was questioned in the XIX century; however, studies by Dodgson (1926) and Flechsig (II, 1931) appear to have established that the work is by Dürer.

An altarpiece devoted to the Virgin (see nos. 12–13) and the *Great Crucifixion* were the two major projects planned by Dürer after his return from the Netherlands. The large number of preparatory studies for the latter—rare in the case of an engraving—indicate the importance of the work in the mind of the artist. More than ten drawings are known in connection with the engraved composition; dated from 1521 to 1523, they are all executed in black chalk on prepared paper. The Louvre claims three further examples of these studies: *Christ upon the Cross* (Inventory RF 60), *Mary Magdalene Kneeling at the Foot of the Cross* (see no. 15) and *Head of a Weeping Cherub* (Inventory 18.589).   A.C.

Albrecht Dürer

1471 - 1528

15. *Mary Magdalene Kneeling at the Foot of the Cross*

TECHNIQUE. Black chalk, heightened with white, on green prepared paper. (29.1 x 20.4 cm.). Dated at lower right: *1523*, with monogram.

PROVENANCE. Th. Lawrence; stamp at lower left (Lugt 2445). H. Defer-Dumesnil; stamp at lower left (Lugt 739); sale, Paris, 1900, no. 37. A. Beurdeley; stamp at lower left (Lugt 421); sale, Paris, 1920, no. 15. Bought at this sale by the Louvre.
Inventory RF 5168.

BIBLIOGRAPHY. Demonts, 1937, vol. I, no. 114, pl. XLIII.
Tietze and Tietze-Conrat, 1938, no. 901, repr. p. 187, fig. 901.
F. Winkler, *Die Zeichnungen Albrecht Dürers*, Berlin, IV, 1939, no. 860, fig. 860.
E. Panofsky, *The Life and Art of Albrecht Dürer*, Princeton, New Jersey, 1948, I, p. 225; II, no. 536, fig. 282.

This is one of the four Louvre drawings related to the engraving known as the *Great Crucifixion* (see no. 14). Two projects for the figure of Saint John are in the Albertina (Winkler, nos. 859 and 875) and seven heads of cherubs are divided among various collections (Winkler, nos. 862–869). The size of these studies is somewhat surprising, as corresponding figures in the engraving would have been considerably smaller. Nonetheless, it seems unlikely they were intended for a painted work, since the group of Holy Women (see no. 14) is placed on the wrong side of the Cross (Panofsky, *op. cit.*, p. 225).

The pathos expressed in the face of Mary Magdalene, the attitude of the body wound around the Cross, contrast with the restrained grief and stiff attitudes of the Holy Women, and as Panofsky appropriately points out, already foreshadow the ecstasies of Baroque art. This is one of the most intense manifestations of Dürer's religious ardor, last expressed in the panel of the *Four Apostles* which he painted in 1526 for the town of Nuremberg (Munich Pinakothek).   A.C.

Lucas Cranach the Elder
1472 - 1558

16. *Portrait of a Man*

TECHNIQUE. Oil on paper. (21.9 x 14.7 cm.). Mount cut in form of an irregular octagon and pasted on a sheet colored brown.

PROVENANCE. F. Flameng; sale, Paris, 1919, no. 12, repr. Bought at this sale by the Louvre.
Inventory RF 4652.

BIBLIOGRAPHY. Demonts, 1937, vol. I, no. 86, pl. XXVIII.
Lucas Cranach d.A. und Lucas Cranach der Jüngere, Exhibition Catalogue, Berlin, 1937, no. 214.
T. L. Girshausen, *Die Handzeichnungen Lucas Cranach d.A*, Frankfort, 1944, no. 93.
J. Rosenberg. *Die Zeichnungen Lucas Cranach d.A.*, Berlin, 1960, no. 88, repr.
Le Seizième Siècle européen. Dessins du Louvre, Exhibition Catalogue, Paris, Louvre, 1965, no. 46, repr.

This famous work establishes Cranach's authority as a portraitist. The lightly sketched garment is briefly indicated and the attention centered entirely on the face. The features are delineated with a precise contour, the modeling is sober, and the look of the eyes remarkably intense. A keen observer, Cranach successfully conveys not only his model's outward appearance, but the essential traits of his character.

Scholars generally agree that this study, executed around 1540, is connected with a series of portraits of members of the family of the Electors of Saxony, now in the Musée des Beaux-Arts in Rheims (Rosenberg, nos. 77–87). When the series was bequeathed to the Rheims Ecole de Dessin, in 1752, by Antoine Ferrand de Monthelon, son of the enamel painter Philippe Ferrand, it comprised, according to an inventory compiled in 1770, seventeen heads incorrectly attributed to Dürer. In 1833, only fifteen pieces from the original series remained in Rheims, and there is reason to believe that both of the missing portraits are now in the Louvre. In addition to the work reproduced, the Louvre has a *Portrait of a Young Man* in the same technique which bears an apocryphal Dürer monogram and the date 1525 added at a later period; however, the initials of Cranach appear on the verso (Inventory 18.870; repr. Demonts, no. 87, pl. XXVIII). R.B.

Albrecht Altdorfer
About 1480 - 1538

17. *Departure for the Witches' Sabbath*

TECHNIQUE. Pen and black ink, heightened with white, on deep beige tinted paper. (17.9 x 12.4 cm.). Dated in pen and ink at lower left: *1506*, with artist's monogram above.

PROVENANCE. Acquired by the Louvre during the Revolution. Inventory 18.867.

BIBLIOGRAPHY. M. J. Friedländer, *Albrecht Altdorfer*, Berlin, 1923, p. 14, repr. p. 13.
Demonts, 1937, vol. I, no. 8, pl. II.
H. L. Becker, *Die Handzeichnungen Albrecht Altdorfers*, Munich, 1938, pp. 5-7, 117, no. 56, pl. I.
F. Winzinger, *Albrecht Altdorfer Zeichnungen*, Munich, 1952, no. 2, pp. 65-66, pl. 2.
Le Seizième Siècle européen. Dessins du Louvre, Exhibition Catalogue, Paris, Louvre, 1965, no. 51, pl. XIV.

The attribution of this remarkable drawing to Altdorfer, suggested by M. Friedländer in 1923, has not been questioned. Not only unanimously accepted as one of the first known drawings by the German master, the Louvre *Witches' Sabbath* is considered one of his major works. The same date, 1506, appears on two other drawings very similar in format and executed in the same technique; one, in the Kupferstichkabinett in Berlin, shows two women lifting a basket of fruit (repr. Winzinger, pl. 1); the other, *Samson and Delilah*, is in the Metropolitan Museum in New York (repr. F. Winzinger, in *Jahrbuch Wien*, Bd. XVIII, fig. 1).

The theme of the Witches' Sabbath enabled Altdorfer to give the full measure of his lyric and visionary genius; in the foreground four half naked witches are seen in expressively animated attitudes; huge clouds surge upward towards the left, carrying in their ascending path a strange cavalcade of figures mounted on fabulous goats, their draperies flying and hair unbound; the real landscape, with a village at the left and a wooded area where the scene transpires has been transformed into a landscape of vision. These elements combine to form an intensely poetic creation, and the artist's decisive pen, his intelligent use of white heightening for emphasis, his chiaroscuro treatment on the colored background reveal the masterly draughtsman. The same fanciful imagination inspires his illustrations for the *Book of Hours of Maximilian I*, in the Besançon Library (repr. Winzinger, pls. 70–95). A work deriving from the *Sabbath* is now in the Budapest Museum (Becker, no. 112).   R.B.

Albrecht Altdorfer

About 1480 - 1538

18. *Two Lansquenets*

TECHNIQUE. Pen and black ink, heightened with white, on brown tinted paper. (19.6 x 14.9 cm.).

PROVENANCE. Acquired by the Louvre before 1827. Inventory 18.919.

BIBLIOGRAPHY. K. T. Parker, *Drawings of the Early German Schools*, London, 1926, no. 60, pl. 60.
Demonts, 1937, vol. I, no. 9, pl. II.
H. L. Becker, *Die Handzeichnungen Albrecht Altdorfers*, Munich, 1938, p. 168.
F. Winzinger, *Albrecht Altdorfer Zeichnungen*, Munich, 1952, no. 119, p. 97, pl. 119.

In 1926, K. T. Parker published the present drawing, previously classified under Wolf Huber, as a work by Albrecht Altdorfer, an attribution maintained by L. Demonts in 1937. It would seem that the rather enigmatic and boldly designed scene is the creation of Altdorfer's original mind and highly personal vision. A man is seen sitting at the foot of a tree with his halberd beside him; at the right, another man is stretched out on the ground, possibly dead. It is difficult to determine the subject—a simple halt or possibly the outcome of a skirmish. A briefly sketched setting in pen and ink is heightened with white to indicate foliage and a distant landscape, while the bend of the trees gives rhythm to the composition—a movement repeated in other drawings by Altdorfer, notably the *Wild Man* and *Saint Jerome*, in the British Museum (repr. Winzinger, pls. 6, 47). The expressive foreshortening of the body lying on the ground is used for the figure in the foreground of the *Wild Family*, dated 1510, in the Albertina (repr. *idem*, pl. 24), and again in the *Death of Pyramus* in the Kupferstichkabinett in Berlin (repr. *idem*, pl. 27). Also typical of Altdorfer's style are the proportions of the figures in relation to the scene as a whole. In fact, though H. L. Becker and F. Winzinger have both expressed doubts concerning the authorship of this drawing, its merits are sufficiently obvious to warrant, here, the attribution to Altdorfer. A copy of this work is also in the Louvre (Inventory 18.926; Demonts, no. 12).   R.B.

Matthias Grünewald

1470/1480 - 1526

19. *Study of an Old Woman*

TECHNIQUE. Black chalk. (20.3 x 15 cm.). Apocryphal Dürer monogram.

PROVENANCE. Probably E. Jabach. The Royal Collection; paraphs of R. de Cotte and A. Coypel (Lugt 1963 and 478).
Inventory 18.588.

BIBLIOGRAPHY. H. A. Schmid, *Die Gemälde und Zeichnungen von Matthias Grüne-wald*, Strasbourg, vol. I, 1907, pl. 49; vol. II, 1911, p. 269.
M. J. Friedländer, *Die Zeichnungen von Matthias Grünewald*, Berlin, 1927, pl. 32.
Demonts, 1937, vol. I, no. 206, pl. LXIX.
W. K. Zülch, *Der historische Grünewald Mathis Gothardt Nithardt*, Munich, 1938, fig. 178.
L. Behling, *Die Handzeichnungen des Mathis Gothart Nithart Gewannt Grüne-wald*, Weimar, 1955, no. 36, pl. XXXIII.

In this portrait of an old woman wearing a bonnet, the black chalk mercilessly records the marks of age, lining the face and neck with furrows; at the same time, it supplely moulds the face in light and shadow and lifts the corners of the mouth in a smile that brightens the eyes. The direct realism of the study is reminiscent of Dürer, to whom it was long assigned; however, the blurred, pictorial treatment and enigmatic expression of the model led M. J. Friedländer to suggest Grünewald as the artist in 1905, an attribution which has remained uncontested. In fact, the work stands out as one of Grünewald's most subtle graphic creations.

The artist appears to have studied the same model in a drawing in the Ashmolean Museum in Oxford for the figure of the Virgin or Mary Magdalene in a *Crucifixion* (repr. K. T. Parker, *Drawings in the Ashmolean Museum*, I, 1938, no. 297, pl. LXII). It is difficult to establish the exact date of the Louvre drawing; scholarly opinions vary: L. Demonts dates it about 1505–1506, while W. K. Zülch classifies it among Grünewald's studies for his famous Isenheim Altarpiece, and L. Behling believes it to be a representative example of the artist's late style.   R.B.

Matthias Grünewald

1470/1480 - 1526

20. *Portrait of Margarethe Prellwitz*

TECHNIQUE. Black chalk, heightened with brown wash, red chalk and white on cream paper. (28.8 x 22.7 cm.). Inscribed in pen and ink on verso: *HANS SCHENICZ MUOTTER*; below: *Margreit brelwiczin*; to the right: *ÆTATIS SUÆ*.

PROVENANCE. Acquired by the Louvre during the Revolution. Inventory 18.936.

BIBLIOGRAPHY. H. Tietze, "The Mother of Hans Schönitz," in *The Burlington Magazine*, 1924, pp. 216-222, repr.
E. Baumeister, "Eine Zeichnung Grünewald," in *Münchner Jahrbuch N. F.*, III, 1926, pp. 269-272, repr.
Demonts, vol. I, 1937, no. 208, pl. LXVIII.
W. K. Zülch, *Der historische Grünewald, Mathis Gothardt Neithardt*, Munich, 1938, p. 338, no. 36.
L. Behling, *Die Handzeichnungen des Mathis Gothart Nithart genannt Grünewald*, Weimar, 1955, no. 37, pl. XXXIV.

In this study the master of the Isenheim Altarpiece reaches one of the high points of his dramatic, expressionistic art. The closed eyes and parted lips of the face framed by the stiffly pleated white bonnet project a striking image of suffering or possibly death. The model, conclusively identified in 1924 by H. Tietze thanks to the inscriptions on the verso of the sheet, is Margarethe Prellwitz, the third wife of Martin Schönitz, a modest citizen of Halle, and mother of the famous Hans Schönitz, who was the right-hand man of Cardinal Albrecht of Brandenburg. The portrait was probably executed toward the end of the artist's career, when he was working at the court of the Cardinal.

The attribution to Grünewald, first suggested in 1926 by E. Baumeister, was maintained with reservations by L. Demonts, who classified the work in 1937 as a drawing in the "Grünewald manner." In more recent studies of the master, W. K. Zülch and L. Behling both acknowledge it to be one of Grünewald's major graphic works and undoubtedly one of the most remarkable creations of the art of the Middle Rhine during the first quarter of the XVI century. R.B.

Hans Baldung Grien
1484/1485 - 1545

21. *Phyllis and Aristotle*

TECHNIQUE. Pen and black ink. (28 x 20.1 cm.). Dated in pen and ink at lower center: *1503*.

PROVENANCE. The Royal Collection; paraph at upper left of R. de Cotte (Lugt 1963).
Inventory 18.865.

BIBLIOGRAPHY. K. T. Parker, "Quelques dessins de Hans Baldung à Paris," in *Archives alsaciennes d'Histoire de l'Art*, III, 1924, p. 18, fig. 12.
Demonts, 1937, vol. I, no. 34, pl. VIII.
F. Winkler, *Hans Baldung Grien*, Burg bei Magdeburg, 1939, no. 1, repr. p. 25.
C. Koch, *Die Zeichnungen Hans Baldung Grien*, Berlin, 1941, pp. 22, 69, Cat. no. 1, pl. I.
Le Seizième Siècle européen. Dessins du Louvre, Exhibition Catalogue, Paris, Louvre, 1965, no. 53, pl. XV.

Phyllis, the courtesan, dressed in the fashion of a XVI century German noblewoman, is seen reins and whip in hand, astride the back of Aristotle, who is walking on all fours. The battlements and towers of a German village rise up at the left.

Here we have one of the themes peculiar to medieval fabliaux and sometimes represented in miniatures and ivories: philosophy reduced to slavery by woman. However, the interest of the drawing lies less in the survival of the moralizing theme than in the savory realism of the notations and the free sweep of the landscape. *Phyllis and Aristotle* was first published as one of Baldung Grien's early works by K. T. Parker, in 1923, an attribution since confirmed by L. Demonts, F. Winkler, and C. Koch. The figure types and calligraphy are clearly influenced by Dürer, who was Baldung Grien's master. In fact, the young Baldung probably executed the drawing, dated 1503, before he was twenty, while still an apprentice in Nuremberg and directly under the influence of Dürer. A similar pen and ink treatment, with alternating cross cuts and supple, expressive lines, characterizes a sheet of studies with seventeen heads, dating from the Nuremberg period (Louvre, Inventory 18.611; repr. Demonts, pl. XI). The Louvre also claims an *Autoportrait* in black chalk, representing the artist at the age of forty-nine (Inventory 18.876, repr. Demonts, pl. X).

R.B.

Hans Holbein the Younger

1497 - 1548

22. *Saint Adrian*

TECHNIQUE. Pen and gray ink, gray wash, heightened with' white, on gray washed paper. (27.8 x 18.8 cm.). Unevenly cut at the upper part; lower corners trimmed.

PROVENANCE. Acquired by the Louvre before 1827.
Inventory 18.944.

BIBLIOGRAPHY. C. Glaser, *Hans Holbein der Jüngere, Zeichnungen*, Basel, 1924, pl. 18.
Demonts, 1937, vol. 1, no. 221, pl. LXXIV.
P. Ganz, *Les Dessins de Hans Holbein le Jeune*, Geneva, 1939, no. 108, p. 34, repr. vol. III, pl. 8.
H. A. Schmid, *Hans Holbein der Jüngere*, Basel, 1948, I, p. 91, pl. 12.
Die Malerfamilie Holbein in Basel, Exhibition Catalogue, Basel, 1960, no. 274, pl. 84.

Saint Adrian is seen standing on a ledge in front of a battlement, holding a sword in his right hand, an anvil in the left; a lion lies at his feet. The manner in which the figure is presented and the "camaieu" treatment against a gray background seem to indicate that this important work was a project for the outside of an altar panel painted in grisaille. The saint carries a Swiss dagger at his waist and is clad in the same armor as Saint Ursus, at the right in the famous altar painting, *The Madonna of Solothurn*, datable 1522 (Exhibition Catalogue, Basel, 1960, no. 163, repr. pl. 71). His stance resembles that of *Saint George* in the altar panel also dating from 1522, the counterpart of *Saint Ursula*, in the Staatliche Kunsthalle in Karlsruhe (*idem*, nos. 164-165). The Louvre study can further be compared to the drawing of *Saint Michael* in Basel (*idem*, no. 258, repr. pl. 89) and to the figure of *Joshua* in a series of wood engravings for the Old Testament (*idem*, nos. 423-30).

The qualities of this drawing—the sober arrangement of the different elements, the skillfully balanced, monumental figure, the vigorous treatment of the gray wash, and finally, the beautiful expression of the face—are evidence of the master's authority as a draughtsman during his period in Basel around 1522, revealing, at the same time, the traces of Northern Italian art in his work.

R.B.

Hans Holbein the Younger

1497 - 1548

23. Three Studies of Hands

TECHNIQUE. Metalpoint, heightened with red chalk; black chalk for the right hand. Gray prepared paper. (20.1 x 15.3 cm.).

PROVENANCE. P. Vischer; sale, Basel, 1852, no. 44; bought at this sale by the Louvre.
Inventory 18.697.

BIBLIOGRAPHY. Demonts, 1937, vol. I, no. 230, pl. LXXIX.
P. Ganz, *Les Dessins de Holbein le Jeune*, Geneva, 1939, I, no. 7, pl. 7.
E. Schilling, *Les Dessins de la famille Holbein*, Paris, 1954, no. 33, repr.
Die Malerfamilie Holbein in Basel, Exhibition Catalogue, Basel, 1960, no. 275.
Le Seizième Siècle européen. Dessins du Louvre, Exhibition Catalogue, Paris, Louvre, 1965, no. 58, pl. XVI.

These are the hands of Erasmus. The artist appears to have made the acquaintance of the famous humanist in 1515, and at the end of that year he illustrated with pen and ink drawings a copy of *The Praise of Folly*, which had recently been reedited (Kupferstichkabinet, Basel). An annotation by Myconius, the book's first owner and a disciple of Erasmus, claims that Holbein's work was known and admired by the humanist. Moreover, the letters of Erasmus testify to the friendly relations enjoyed by the two men in Basel, in 1523. It was during this period that Holbein executed the three portraits of his illustrious friend, which are now in the Louvre, the Radnor Collection in Longford Castle, and the Basel Museum (repr. A. Gerlo, *Erasme et ses portraitistes*, Brussels, 1950, pls. IX-XI). The Louvre and Basel paintings show Erasmus writing, turned to the left in profile; in the Longford Castle canvas he is facing three-quarters left, with his hands resting on a book. In the present sheet, the two metalpoint studies for the left hand, heightened with red chalk, are connected with the latter painting. The right hand holding the pen and drawn in black chalk is believed to be a study for the Louvre and Basel paintings; however, the authenticity of this particular sketch has sometimes been questioned. For the Longford portrait, the Louvre claims another drawing in the same technique for the right hand, which, like the drawing reproduced, was bought at the Vischer sale in Basel in 1852 (Inventory 18.698; repr. Demonts, pl. LXXIX). These remarkable studies indicate the keenness of Holbein's observations and his objectivity before the model, as well as the particular care with which he executed his portraits of Erasmus. They also represent a moving testimony of the meeting of two great figures of the European Renaissance, who were to embody some of the most essential aspects of their period.   R. B.

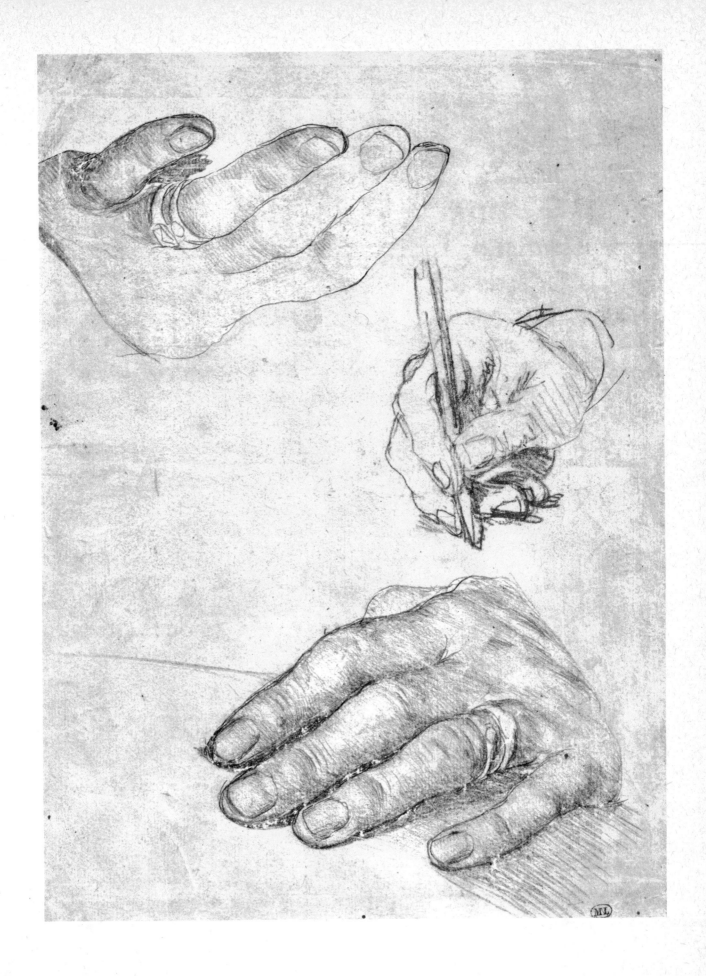

Hans Holbein the Younger

1497 - 1548

24. *Portrait of a Young Woman*

TECHNIQUE. Metalpoint, contours reworked by the artist in pen and black ink, heightened with red chalk and white, on pink prepared paper. (19.6 x 15.4 cm.). The young woman's bodice is bordered in capital letters: *ALS. IN. ERN. ALS. IN.* Verso: light sketch of a man's face, turned to the left in profile.

PROVENANCE. E. Jabach; paraph on verso (Lugt 2959). Purchased for the Royal Collection in 1671.
Inventory 20.737.

BIBLIOGRAPHY. Demonts, 1937, vol. I, no. 228, pl. LXXVIII.
P. Ganz, *Les Dessins de Hans Holbein le Jeune*, Geneva, 1939, no. 5, p. 2, repr. vol. I, pl. 5.
K. Scheffer, *Dessins de Hans Holbein le Jeune*, Paris, 1944, pl. 8.
Die Malerfamilie Holbein in Basel, Exhibition Catalogue, Basel, 1960, no. 255.
Le Seizième Siècle européen. Dessins du Louvre, Exhibition Catalogue, Paris, Louvre, 1965, no. 56, pl. XV.

In the XVII century this drawing belonged to the connoisseur Everard Jabach, who classified it with the "rebut" of his collection. When it entered the Royal Collection in 1671, it was first inventoried among the Italian works and then with the German school of the XVI century, before being finally attributed to Holbein the Younger. Now considered one of the most beautiful of the master's youthful drawings, it is believed by most scholars to be a study for the Virgin in the painting known as the *Madonna of Solothurn*, executed in 1522 for Johann Gerster, the town registrar, and now in the Solothurn Museum (Exhibiton Catalogue, Basel, 1960, no. 163, repr. pl. 71).

A single metalpoint line serves to delineate the curve of the shoulders, to model the rounded cheeks and detail the braided hair, with its few stray wisps. An impression of youth radiating from the inclined face is further heightened by the faint half-smile lighting up the eyes from beneath lowered lids. Around her throat the young woman wears the emblem of the order of Saint Anthony—probably a charm against the plague; on her bodice a motto is embroidered, which has been deciphered to read: *All in honor.* In the painting, the woman's face is raised and the smiling expression somewhat attenuated. It is likely that the artist's model was his wife, Elsbeth Binzenstock, who is represented in the *Family Portrait* in the Basel Museum, executed about 1528-1529. In the latter work she is older and her features more marked, but the conformation of the eyes is easily recognized (*idem*, no. 180, repr. pl. 73).   R. B.

Hans Holbein the Younger
1497 - 1548

25. *Decoration for the Facade of a House*

TECHNIQUE. Pen and gray ink, gray and blue wash. (58.2 x 27.5 cm.).

PROVENANCE. E. Jabach; paraphs on verso of gilt bordered mount (Lugt 2959 and 2953) with the number: *trois cent six*. Purchased for the Royal Collection in 1671.
Inventory 18.696.

BIBLIOGRAPHY. A. Woltman, *Holbein und seine Zeit*, Leipzig, vol. I, 1874, p. 148; vol. II, 1876, no. 235, p. 146.
V. Champier, *Musée du Louvre. Modèles d'art décoratif*, Paris, 1882, pl. XXIX.
Ed. His, *Dessins d'ornements de Hans Holbein*, Paris, 1886, pls. XVIII, XX.
Demonts, 1937, vol. I, no. 231, pl. LXXXI.
Le Seizième Siècle européen. Dessins du Louvre, Paris, Exhibition Catalogue, Louvre, 1965, no. 229, pl. LIX.

This important work, already attributed to Holbein in the handwritten inventory of the Jabach Collection acquired by Louis XIV in 1671 (Ecole d'Allemagne, no. 306) retains all the freshness of its colored highlights, while affording a noteworthy example of the ease and inventiveness displayed by the artist in his studies for decorative works. In this project for a facade, he gives free expression to his lively narrative bent, combining motifs imaginatively reinterpreted from Classical art with colorful and realistic notations. On the friezes, figures with bodies trailing off in arabesques struggle or embrace; at the base, two dogs quarrel over a bone, while in the upper part, giants are seen trying to squeeze through twin columns.

It is interesting to compare this decorative style, highly representative of the Renaissance movement in Northern Europe, with the projects for facades elaborated by certain Italian masters like Perino del Vaga and Polidoro da Caravaggio, who worked in the entourage of Raphael, or Pordenone and other Venetians. The date of the drawing can be roughly established on the basis of a similarity in style and technique with other projects for facades executed by Holbein in Switzerland between 1517 and 1524, in particular for the Hartenstein House in Lucerne (P. Ganz, *Les Dessins de Hans Holbein le Jeune*, Geneva, 1939, no. 112, repr. vol. III, pl. 12) and for the *Zum Tanz* House in Basel (*idem*, nos. 113, 114, repr. vol. III, pls. 13, 14). Holbein created a type of stained glass window considered one of the major achievements of the Northern Renaissance; he was to develop his decorative talents in England, in the service of Henry VIII, in studies of jewels, arms and various curios, among which the famous *Project for an Astronomical Clock*, a drawing which was presented to the King in 1544 and is now in the British Museum (*idem*, no. 220, repr. vol. V, pl. 220).   R. B.

Hans Holbein the Younger

1497 - 1548

26. *Portrait of Thomas Wriothesley, Earl of Southampton*

TECHNIQUE. Black and colored chalk, reworked by the artist in pen and black ink on pink tinted paper. (24.3 x 19.4 cm.). Cut along the contours and pasted on a sheet tinted with red chalk.

PROVENANCE. J. Richardson, Senior; stamp at lower right (Lugt 2183); paraph on verso (Lugt 2984). Fairfax Murray. F. Flameng; sale, Paris, 1919, no. 61. Bought at this sale by the Louvre.
Inventory RF 4651.

BIBLIOGRAPHY. C. S. Wortley, "The Portrait of Thomas Wriothesley Earl of Southampton, by Holbein," in *The Burlington Magazine*, 1930, p. 85, repr. p. 82, fig. B.
Demonts, 1937, vol. I, no. 224, pl. LXXVI.
P. Ganz, *Les Dessins de Hans Holbein le Jeune*, Geneva, 1939, no. 87, p. 27, repr. vol. III, pl. 36.
A. Hulftegger, *Les Dessins de Holbein*, Paris, 1950, pl. 8.
Le Seizième Siècle européen. Dessins du Louvre, Exhibition Catalogue, Paris, Louvre, 1965, no. 57, pl. XV.

1532 marked for Holbein the beginning of a brilliant new period of uninterrupted activity in England, which lasted until his death in London in 1548. The prestige he enjoyed as a portraitist can be gauged by the large number of distinguished figures who sat for him. There are famous drawn portraits or studies of such high ranking personages as Anne Boleyn, in 1533, shortly after her marriage to Henry VIII (Earl of Bradford Collection; repr. Ganz, vol. I, pl. 39), Jane Seymour, in 1536 (Windsor; repr. *idem*, pl. 44), or the future Edward VI as a child (repr. *idem*, pls. 47-49).

During this period, Holbein simplified his working methods, using black and colored chalks on white paper primed with pale pink; in a few strokes a resemblance is captured and the model graced with a singular presence. The drawing reproduced is a remarkable example of the group of portraits executed in England between 1532 and 1548; the subject is Thomas Wriothesley (1500-1550), one of the most prominent figures in the court of Henry VIII. In 1538, he accompanied the diplomatic mission sent to Mary, the Regent of the Netherlands, to negotiate the king's marriage to Christina, the Duchess of Milan; in 1544, he became Chancellor of England, and in 1547, received the title of Earl of Southampton. A miniature version of Wriothesley's portrait, showing him in the same position, was drawn by Holbein on a playing card which is now in the Metropolitan Museum in New York (B. Burroughs, "A Miniature by Holbein," in the *Bulletin of the Metropolitan Museum*, 1926, p. 98); two painted versions of the portrait belong to the collections of Lord Montagu of Beaulieu and the Duke of Bedford (repr. C. S. Wortley, figs. C and D).

R. B.

Hans Holbein the Younger

1497 - 1548

27. *The Triumph of Wealth*

TECHNIQUE. Pen and brown ink, brown wash, heightened with white, on beige paper. (25.1 x 56.9 cm.). Squared up in black chalk. The names of the figures are inscribed in pen and ink.

PROVENANCE. E. Jabach; paraphs on verso (Lugt 2959 and 2953) and the number: *vingt trois*. Purchased for the Royal Collection in 1671. Inventory 18.694.

BIBLIOGRAPHY. Demonts, 1937, vol. I, no. 223, pl. LXXV.
P. Ganz, *Les Dessins de Hans Holbein le Jeune*, Geneva, 1939, no. 120, p. 40, repr. vol. III, pl. 120.
F. Grossmann, "Holbein, Flemish Paintings and Everard Jabach," in *The Burlington Magazine*, 1951, p. 22.
L' Europe Humaniste, Exhibition Catalogue, Brussels, 1954-1955, no. 92, pl. 80.
Le Seizième Siècle européen. Dessins du Louvre, Exhibition Catalogue, Paris, Louvre, 1965, no. 55, pl. XV.

This project was elaborated for one of the compositions adorning the Banquet Hall in the Steelyard House in London, which belonged to the merchants of the Hanseatic League. The procession of the *Triumph of Wealth* is shown advancing toward the left, headed by allegorical figures leading four horses; the horses draw the chariot upon which are seated Fortune, unfurling her veil and scattering gold coins, and Pluto, beneath a canopy. Those blessed with wealth, whose names have come down in history and legend, escort the chariot, while, to the right, Nemesis hovers in the upper regions. A second panel, completing the Steelyard decoration, showed the *Triumph of Poverty*. At the beginning of the XVII century the paintings were presented to the Prince of Wales; they later entered the collections of King Charles I and the Earl of Arundel, and at the end of the XVII century, are mentioned as being in Paris, where their trace is lost.

The significance of these works and their importance in Holbein's evolution were studied by H. Koegler in 1933. Painted or engraved copies give us an idea of what they were like, notably the engraving, *Triumph of Wealth*, dated 1561 and published by Jean Borigiani in Antwerp (repr. P. Ganz, *H. Holbein*, Stuttgart-Leipzig, 1912, p. 175). The Louvre *Triumph*, which belonged to Jabach before entering the Royal Collection in 1671, is also a rare and valuable testimony of the mural decorations executed by Holbein while he was in England. The format and technique, as well as the frieze design, elicit comparison with *Samuel Cursing King Saul*, a project for one of the decorations in the Basel Town Hall, executed about 1529–1530 (Basel; repr. Ganz, vol. III, pl. 18); however, the more mature Louvre drawing is stylistically of exceptional interest for its beautifully rhythmed composition and masterful draughtsmanship.   R.B.

Jost Amman
1539 - 1591

28. *Saint Nicholas*

TECHNIQUE. Pen and black ink, heightened with white, on red prepared paper. (30.1 x 19.7 cm.). Signed at lower approximate center with the initials, *J. A.*, and dated, *1588*.

PROVENANCE. Probably E. Jabach. The Royal Collection; paraph of Robert de Cotte at upper left (Lugt 1963).
Inventory 18.498.

BIBLIOGRAPHY. P. Ganz, *Handzeichnungen Schweizerischer Meister des XV-XVIII Jahrhunderts*, Basel (1904-1908), vol. III, pl. 58.
Demonts, 1937, vol. I, no. 15, pl. III.
A. P. de Mirimonde, "Les Sujets de musique dans les œuvres allemandes du Musée du Louvre," in *Revue du Louvre*, 1964, 3, p. 128, fig. 28.
Le Seizième Siècle européen. Dessins du Louvre, Exhibition Catalogue, Paris, Louvre, 1965, no. 62, pl. XVI.

This savory and somewhat unusual image of Saint Nicholas, which belonged to the Royal Collection, shows him as the protector of big eaters, dressed as a *Vielgrass*, that is to say, a glutton. A wealth of colorful and lively details depict him jogging along on a donkey, waving a *Buckelglas* in his left hand. His waist is tied with a string of bells, his head strangely adorned with a small shrub harboring a bird's nest and laden with roast chicken, sausages and fish. In his study of this drawing in 1964, A. P. de Mirimonde points out that Saint Nicholas was already described jingling small bells as early as the XIII century. The interest of the work, which has the direct appeal of a popular image, is heightened by the quality of the interpretation: the placement of the motif is felicitous; a decorative effect is achieved through the use of a colored background and the precision of the artist's pen which delights in minute details and whimsical arabesques. The concise draughtsmanship is reminiscent of Amman's activity as an engraver on copper and wood, known primarily for his illustrations of the *Book of Labors*, by Hans Sachs.

Melchior Lorch

1525 - 1586(?)

29. *Dromedary Carrying a Kettledrummer*

TECHNIQUE. Pen and ink, brown wash. (33.1 x 47.1 cm.). Inscribed in pen and ink at upper right: *Camele die Türkischen Kaisers Schätztrager* and signed with a monogram composed of intertwined letters *ML*, written over with *F*, cutting across the date *1557*. In pen and ink toward the lower right: *1577*(?).

PROVENANCE. Acquired by the Louvre during the Revolution. Inventory 18.727.

BIBLIOGRAPHY. Demonts, 1937, vol. I, no. 260, pl. XCV.
A. P. de Mirimonde, "Les Sujets de musique dans les œuvres allemandes du Musée du Louvre," in *Revue du Louvre*, 1964, no. 3, p. 127, fig. 27.
Le Seizième Siècle européen. Dessins du Louvre, Exhibition Catalogue, Paris, Louvre, 1965, no. 209, pl. LIV.

Few of the many drawings made by Lorch during the course of his adventurous life have come down to us, which makes the *Dromedary* one of his most important works in museum collections (*Melchior Lorch. Drawings from the Evelyn Collection at Stonor Park, England, and from the Department of Prints and Drawings. The Royal Museum of Fine Arts*, Exhibition Catalogue, Copenhagen, 1962). The lightly sketched landscape evokes the distant regions to which the artist travelled between 1555 and 1560, when he accompanied the diplomatic mission sent by Emperor Ferdinand II to Sultan Soliman I, to arbitrate the conflict over the control of Transylvania. Probably drawn during this trip and finished at a later date, as certain historians suggest, the drawing offers a witty example of Lorch's fantasy and original style (see also *Study of a Tortoise*, dated 1555, in the British Museum). Moreover, the freedom of his pen, the sureness and balance of the composition, stripped of all anecdotal detail, prefigure the XVIII century use of Oriental motifs in decoration.

The same subject reappears in a 1576 engraving in the *Turkish Costumes* series (Nagler, *Monogrammisten*, IV, p. 616, no. 36).

A. C.

Adam Elsheimer

1578 - 1610

30. *Nocturnal Landscape*

TECHNIQUE. Black and white gouache on reddish brown prepared paper. (8.7 x 15.5 cm.). Inscription on the verso of an old mount: *Adam Elsheimer de Francfort, venant de la vente de M. Mariette*.

PROVENANCE. P. J. Mariette; sale, Paris, 1775, no. 920. Prince de Conti; sale, Paris, 1777, no. 1004. Purchased for the Royal Collection. Inventory 18.658.

BIBLIOGRAPHY. H. Weizsacker, *Adam Elsheimer, der Maler von Frankfurt*, Berlin, 1936, vol. I, no. 163, pl. 145; vol. II, p. 254.
Demonts, vol. II, 1938, no. 554, pl. CXLV.
H. Möhle, *Die Zeichnungen Adam Elsheimers. Das Werk des Meisters und der Problemkreis Elsheimer Goudt*, Berlin, 1966, p. 46, fig. 28.
Adam Elsheimer Werk, künstlerische Herkunft und Nachfolge, Exhibition Catalogue, Frankfort, 1966-1967, no. 148, pl. 129.
Le Cabinet d'un grand amateur, P. J. Mariette, Exhibition Catalogue, Paris, Louvre, 1967, no. 173.

After working in his native town of Frankfort and then in Venice, from 1600 on Elsheimer settled in Rome where he made the acquaintance of Paul Bril. In the field of landscape representation he had a considerable influence on his contemporaries; furthermore, he is the direct forerunner of some of the great landscape painters of the XVII century, as evidenced by the highly pictorial technique of the present drawing and the dreamy melancholy pervading a scene in which figures are purely accessory. Without the Frankfort painter, the art of Rembrandt, who knew Elsheimer through Goudt and Lastman, or that of Claude, is scarcely conceivable. During his short Roman period he was the first to express the modern conception of a landscape attuned to a dominant mood.

Carefully and concisely treated, its twilight atmosphere infused with a lyric quality, this small drawing, which Môhle dates 1605 and compares with a gouache representing *Venus and Cupid in a Landscape* (former Koenigs Collection, Haarlem; repr. fig. 34), is representative of the artist's style during the last years of his career. Gouache drawings of landscapes were rare in Elsheimer's work, and most of those known (Rennes and Berlin Museums; British Museum; Victoria and Albert Museum) are subject to controversy; the Louvre drawing, alone, escapes criticism, again confirming the enlightened taste of its XVIII century owner, Mariette.   A.C.

Hans Rottenhammer
1564 - 1625

31. *Project for the Decoration of a Cup*

TECHNIQUE. Pen and brown ink, brown wash, with certain contours reworked by the artist in pen and black ink. Circular band: 16 cm. wide x 55.6 cm. in diameter. Several pieces of paper pasted together.

PROVENANCE. The Royal Collection; paraphs of R. de Cotte (Lugt 1963) and A. Coypel (Lugt 478).
Inventory 18.766.

BIBLIOGRAPHY. R. A. Peltzer, "Hans Rottenhammer," in *Jahrbuch Wien*, XXXIII, 5, 1916, p. 359, no. 67.
Demonts, vol. II, 1938, no. 666, pl. CLXIII (detail).
H. Bardon, *Le Festin des Dieux*, Paris, 1960, p. 35, note 1.
Le Seizième Siècle européen. Dessins du Louvre, Exhibition Catalogue, Paris, Louvre, 1965, no. 261, pl. LXXI.

After working until the age of twenty-five in Munich, his birthplace, Rottenhammer established himself in Venice from 1589 to 1606. Thanks to his prolonged stay in Italy, this artist, nurtured in the Germanic tradition, was able to experience the great lessons of Italian painting. In the works executed after his return to Munich and later in Augsburg, where he died in 1625, he achieved a successful synthesis of the elements of Northern and Italian art, in a development parallel to that of the Netherlandish Mannerists with whom he no doubt had frequent contact.

This important project for the decoration of a cup, which entered the Royal Collection in the XVII century, depicts two versions of the *Banquet of the Gods*, linked by the representation of a *Naval Victory*. The artist's ease in adapting the organization of these scenes to the circular composition, the full, supple feminine figures and fresh touches of light colored wash create a lively ensemble of particular interest in the history of German Mannerism. The work can be compared to a similar project in the same technique and style representing the *Victory of Venice over the Turks*, now in Düsseldorf (repr. I, Budde, *Beschreibender Katalog der Handzeichnungen in der Staatlichen Kunstakademie*, Düsseldorf, 1930, no. 947, pl. 220).   R.B.

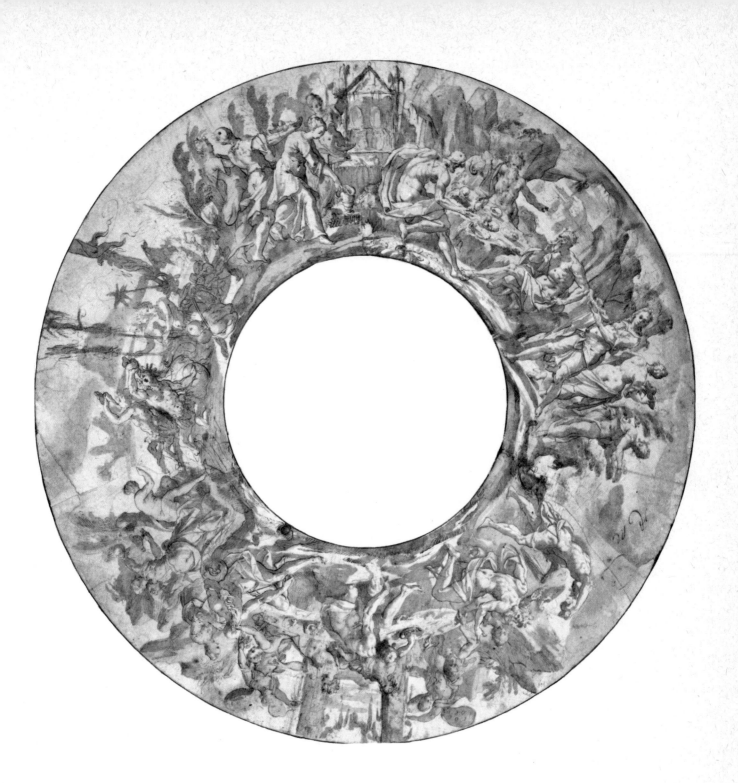

Franz - Xavier - Karl Palcko

1724 - 1767

32. *The Miraculous Oil Oozing from the Tomb of Saint Nicholas, Bishop of Myra*

TECHNIQUE. Pen and brown ink, brown and gray wash over pencil lines. (25.8 x 19.2 cm.).

PROVENANCE. P. J. Mariette; stamp at lower center (Lugt 1852) and mounted with: *FRANC. XAVER PALCKO SILESIUS* inscribed in a cartouche; above: *Tumulo B. Nicolai deo salutari fluente curantur morbi, daemonia ejiciuntur, mortui resurgunt*; sale, Paris, 1775, part of lot no. 972. Bought at this sale for the Royal Collection.
Inventory 18.741.

BIBLIOGRAPHY. K. Garzarolli-Thurnlack, *Die barock Handzeichnungen in Österreich*, Zurich-Vienna-Leipzig, n.d. (1928), p. 84.
Demonts, 1938, no. 634, pl. CLIX.
K. Garas, "Zu einigen Problemen der Malerei des 18. Jahrhunderts. Die Malerfamilie Palko," in *Acta Historiae Artium, Academiae Scientiarum Hungaricae*, vol. VII, Budapest, 1961, pp. 241-244, 247, fig. 5.
Le Cabinet d'un grand amateur, P. J. Mariette, Exhibition Catalogue, Paris, Louvre, 1967, no. 189.

According to the *Golden Legend*, Saint Nicholas, the Bishop of Myra, was buried in Bari; from his marble sarcophagus oozed a miraculous oil which healed the sick who passed under the tomb. This was a project for Palcko's first major work, the cupola in the Jesuit church in Prague dedicated to Saint Nicholas, which he executed in collaboration with his assistants Josef Hager and Josef Redelmayer. In addition to the present drawing, which can be dated with some precision between 1752-1753, at a time when the artist was working at the Dresden court, the Louvre owns a second study connected with the same decoration and previously owned by Mariette (Inventory 18.741). Both are brilliant compositions, whose lively treatment and luminosity reveal the influence of contemporary Venetian art, as well as the artist's evolution towards a decidedly Rococo style—a tendency which is also apparent in works by Maulbertsch or Bergl during the same period. Mariette particularly valued these drawings, obtained from the artist's widow: "Ils sont de la plus grande manière, et je ne regrette point le haut prix qu'ils m'ont coûté. Je n'en ai peu dans ma collection qui me satisfassent autant…" (*Abecedario*, IV, p. 72).   A.C.

Anton Raphael Mengs

1728 - 1779

33. *The Presentation of the Virgin*

TECHNIQUE. Black chalk, heightened with white, on blue-gray paper. (51.2 x 38.7 cm.). Squared up in black chalk. In the lower part, various sketches and inscriptions in black chalk and pen and ink.

PROVENANCE. Purchased by the Louvre from the heirs of the artist before 1827. Inventory 18.738.

BIBLIOGRAPHY. Demonts, vol. II, 1938, no. 617, pl. CLVII.

Mengs is one of the outstanding figures of XVIII century European art, both as an artist and a theoretician of neoclassicism. Born in Aussig in Bohemia, he studied under his father, the painter Ismael Mengs. From 1741–1744, the adolescent Mengs was already living in Rome, where he worked with Marco Benefial and discovered Classical beauty and the great masters of the Italian Renaissance. After his return to Germany, he entered the service of Augustus III, the Elector of Saxony and King of Poland, in Dresden, and remained there until 1746, when he established himself in Rome. Association with Winkelmann, of whom he made a portrait, now in the Metropolitan Museum in New York, strengthened his resolve to return to a noble style in painting which would strive for Classic simplicity and be patterned on the great examples of the past.

After completing the *Parnassus* fresco in the Villa Albani, Mengs went to Spain, at the request of Charles III, and received important commissions for decorative works, in particular for Aranjuez Palace and the Escurial. The drawing reproduced is a preparatory study for the *Presentation of the Virgin*, an altar painting executed in 1758 for Maria-Amalia of Saxony, daughter of Augustus III, and placed in the chapel of Caserte Castle, where it has remained (D. Honisch, *Anton Raphael Mengs und die Bildform des Frühklassizismus*, Recklinghausen, 1965, no. 78, p. 86). The well-balanced composition, the fullness of the forms and beauty of the treatment in black chalk against a colored background testify to the quality of Meng's graphic works, which are too often ignored. This sheet and an *Adoration of the Shepherds* (Inventory 18.737; Demonts, no. 618, repr. pl. CLVII) were purchased by the Louvre directly from the heirs of the artist.   R.B.

Roger van der Weyden

1399/1400 - 1464

34. *Head of the Virgin*

TECHNIQUE. Silverpoint on prepared paper. (12.9 x 1 cm.). Inscribed in pen and ink at lower right: *albert durer*.

PROVENANCE. Acquired by the Louvre during the Revolution.
Inventory 20.644.

BIBLIOGRAPHY. F. Winkler, *Der Meister von Flémalle und Rogier van der Weyden*, Strasbourg, 1913, p. 56, Cat. p. 174, no. 625, pl. 11.
A. E. Popham, *Drawings of the Early Flemish School*, London, 1926, no. 13, repr.
M. J. Friedländer, "A Drawing by Roger van der Weyden," in *Old Master Drawings*, December, 1926, p. 32.
Jules Destrées, *Roger de la Pasture, Van der Weyden*, Paris-Brussels, 1930, p. 190, pl. 150.

Roger de la Pasture, a native of Tournai who worked in Brussels for roughly thirty years and became known as Roger van der Weyden, was regarded almost as highly by his contemporaries as Van Eyck. One of the most significant artists of his time, his influence extended beyond the borders of his own country to both Germany and France. Today his painted works are again becoming well known, though the same is not true of his rare drawings; this precious sheet is one of the very few Van der Weyden studies considered authentic. The technique and careful execution recall the figures of Van Eyck, though here, something more subtly spiritual lights up the tender, melancholy expression of the Virgin. This idealized figure, a young woman of eminent distinction, reappears in several of the artist's paintings representing the Madonna, and is treated with similar delicacy and refinement, notably in the *Virgin and Child*, formerly in the collection of the Prince of Furstenberg in Donaueschingen (repr. M. J. Friedländer, *Die Altniederländische Malerei*, 1934, II, pl. LXVII), of which other versions are known, or again in *Saint Luke Painting the Portrait of the Virgin* (Munich, Boston and Leningrad; repr. Friedländer, pl. LXXIII).   A.C.

Gerard David

About 1455 - 1523

35. *Studies*

TECHNIQUE. Silverpoint on white prepared paper. (9 x 9.7 cm.). Verso: head of a man in black chalk, facing three quarters left. Inscribed in pen and ink at upper left: *XXXIII*.

PROVENANCE. Ph. Dräxler von Carin, until 1874. J. C. von Klinkosch; sale, Vienna, 1889, no. 468, repr. A. von Lanna, Prague; sale, Stuttgart, 1910, no. 199, repr. Bought at this sale by the Louvre.
Inventory RF 3812.

BIBLIOGRAPHY. M. Conway, "Drawings by Gerard David," in *The Burlington Magazine*, XIII, 1908, p. 155, repr. p. 156, pl. I.
P. Leprieur, "De Quelques dessins nouveaux au Musée du Louvre," in *Revue de l' Art Ancien et Moderne*, XXVIII, 1910, pp. 170-171, fig. 4.
F. Winkler, "Das Skizzenbuch Gerard Davids," in *Pantheon*, III, 1929, pp. 271-275, figs. 1 (recto) and 6 (verso).
Le Seizième Siècle européen. Dessins du Louvre, Exhibition Catalogue, Paris, Louvre, 1965, no. 65, pl. XVII.

Taking up the hypothesis of J. Meder (*Handzeichnungen Alter Meister aus der Albertina und anderen Sammlungen*, Bd. 12, 1908, no. 1407, repr.) and P. Leprieur, F. Winkler has shown that this sheet of very delicately drawn studies was part of a series of drawings in the same technique now divided among various museums (Louvre, Frankfort, Cracow, Hamburg...); originally, according to F. Winkler, they probably formed an album. Attributed first to Holbein the Younger and then to the French school of the XV century, the sheets, containing only portraits of men and women, are now acknowledged as authentic works by Gerard David. F. Winkler maintains that this artist may also be the author of the study on the verso of the present sheet, although M. J. Friedländer attributes it to the master of the Brandon portraits (*Gentse Bijdragen tot de Kunst-geschiedenis*, IV, 1937, p. 11). A.C.

36. *Portrait of a Young Girl, Shown to the Waist, and Facing Three Quarters Left*

TECHNIQUE. Silverpoint on prepared paper. (9.5 x 6.5 cm.).

PROVENANCE. Probably the Royal Collection.
Inventory 20.649.

BIBLIOGRAPHY. P. Leprieur, "De Quelques dessins nouveaux au Musée du Louvre," in *Revue de l' Art Ancien et Moderne*, XXVIII, 1910, pp. 172-173, repr. p. 173, fig. 5.
A. E. Popham, *Drawings of the Early Flemish School*, London, 1926, no. 30, repr.
F. Winkler, "Das Skizzenbuch Gerard Davids," in *Pantheon*, III, 1929, pp. 271-275, fig. 5.

In style and technique this small drawing belongs to the same group as the study above. The young girl is set against a flower-strewn background; her delicately drawn face, rendered by a fine light line, has the frail quality and reserved expression common to this series of drawn portraits. Gerard David's paintings are still rooted in XV century tradition; but the sincere and sensitive interpretation of the human face that characterizes his drawn studies is premonitory of the portraits of the following century. A.C.

Hans Memling
About 1433 - 1494

37. *Head of a Saint*

TECHNIQUE. Distemper and gouache on red tinted paper. (22.1 x 16.8 cm.). Inscribed in pen and ink on recto and verso.

PROVENANCE. J. Pz. Zoomer; stamp at lower left (Lugt 1511). W. Mayor. Purchased by the Louvre in 1852.
Inventory 20.053.

BIBLIOGRAPHY. K. Voll, *Memling*, 1909, pl. XXXII.
L. Demonts, *Musée National du Louvre. Catalogue des Peintures exposées dans les Galeries III, Ecoles flamande, hollandaise, allemande et anglaise*, Paris, 1922, p. 50, no. 2028A.
A. E. Popham, *Drawings of the Early Flemish School*, London, 1926, no. 19, repr.

Hans Memling, a German who made Flanders his home, opposes a serene, reserved mysticism to Van Eyck's vigor and Van der Weyden's power and sense of the dramatic, in calm, well-balanced paintings peopled with Madonnas, saints and smiling children. At times, however, the truth of his figures is uncompromising, as in the present drawing, in which the sharpness of line is intensely spiritual. This *Saint's Head* is usually related to the central panel of the triptych commissioned in 1484 by the Moreel family, now in the Communal Museum in Bruges, which represents *Saint Christopher between Saint Maurus and Saint Giles* (repr. M. J. Friedländer, *Die altniederländische Malerei, VI, Memling und Gerard David*, Leyden, 1934, pl. XIV). Believed to be a preliminary sheet for the figure of Saint Maurus at the left, the face studied here, with its tormented expression, also bears a close resemblance to Saint Joseph in the *Adoration of the Magi* in the Prado (repr. *idem*, pl. I), datable about 1470.   A.C.

Bernard van Orley

1492/1495 - 1542

38. *Landscape*

In the left background, a village; in the foreground a woman is seated at the foot of a tree with a child and a man is seen pursuing a woman.

TECHNIQUE. Pen and brown ink, brown wash, heightened with white. (30.9 x 46.1 cm.). Inscribed in pen and ink at lower left: *Meester Bernaet Orlay van Brussel fecit*.

PROVENANCE. P. Crozat; sale, Paris, 1741, part of lot no. 799. P. J. Mariette; stamp at lower right (Lugt 1852) and mounted with: *BERN. VAN ORLEY BRUXELLENSIS* inscribed in a cartouche; sale, Paris, 1775, part of lot no. 968. Bought at this sale for the Royal Collection.
Inventory 20.148.

BIBLIOGRAPHY. *Exposition Universelle et Internationale de Bruxelles. Cinq siècles d' Art*, Exhibition Catalogue, Brussels, 1935, no. 420.
Le Seizième Siècle européen. Dessins du Louvre, Exhibition Catalogue, Paris, Louvre, 1965, no. 68, pl. XVIII.

The Louvre has two more drawings by Van Orley (Inventory 20.147, 20.149) which belonged to Mariette in the XVIII century and, with the present one, comprise a series of three works, each showing a landscape with a picturesque scene in the foreground; possibly they were, as Mariette believed, designs for tapestries. The characteristics of the drawing reproduced are shared by a series of *Hunting Scenes* (see no. 39) in which landscape plays an important part: nature is realistically observed and precisely depicted by the line of the artist's pen; atmosphere is rendered with sensitivity thanks to a fluid and luminous wash thereby justifying the opinion of the famous collector concerning the drawings in his collection: "L'on y trouve des parties de paysages que le Titien ne désavouerait pas" (*Abecedario*, V, p. 392).

In the background of the present drawing can be seen the village of Etterbeck, near Brussels, again represented in a painting in Vienna, the *Flight into Egypt* (*Katalog der Gemäldegalerie Kunsthistorisches Museum*, Vienna, 1928, p. 38, no. 766). With this beautiful landscape and the cartoons for the *Hunting Scenes* Van Orley reveals himself a forerunner of Poussin and Claude Lorrain and an important figure in the development of landscape painting.

A.C.

Bernard van Orley

1492/1495 - 1542

39. *The Stag Hunt*

TECHNIQUE. Pen and brown ink, blue wash. (39.8 x 56.8 cm.).

PROVENANCE. E. Jabach; paraphs on verso of gilt bordered mount (Lugt 2959 and 2953). Purchased for the Royal Collection in 1671.
Inventory 20.154.

BIBLIOGRAPHY. A. Wauters, *Bernard van Orley*, Paris, 1893, repr. p. 83.
P. Alfassa, "Les Tapisseries des Chasses de Maximilien," in *Gazette des Beaux-Arts*, 1920, I, p. 246, repr.
G. Migeon, *Musée du Louvre: Les Tapisseries des Chasses de Maximilien*, Paris, 1920, p. 12, repr.
N. Beets, "Zestiende eeuyusche Kunstenaers II. Barend von Orley Twee eigenhandige Antwerpen von Barend von Orley voor de Tapijtserie der Belles Chasses de Maximilien," in *Oud Holland*, XL, VIII, 1931, p. 147, fig. 3.
Le Seizième Siècle européen. Dessins du Louvre, Exhibition Catalogue, Paris, Louvre, 1965, no. 227, pl. LIX.

Van Orley's talents were no doubt most fully expressed in his cartoons for tapestries, where his art achieves an almost classic breadth and ease. Among those belonging to the Louvre, the most significant may be the twelve small cartoons (Inventory 20.151–20.162) connected with the famous hangings representing *Maximilian's Hunts* also in the Louvre (for the origin of these tapestries see *Le Seizième Siècle européen. Tapisseries*, Exhibition Catalogue, Paris, Mobilier National, 1965, no. 24). Generally dated between 1521 and 1533, or four of five years before the execution of the tapestries, these projects, including the one reproduced, present a double interest: Van Orley displays exceptional creative talent in his conjured-up scenes of imaginary hunts; for the artists coming after him, he opened new paths to Italianism, thereby transforming the conception of the landscape, which he rendered with remarkable truth and spontaneity.

The present cartoon is for the seventh tapestry, representing the sequence of the stag hunt in the forest of Soignes: two huntsmen and the dogs are seen surrounding the animal who has leapt into the Val Vert pond. The realistically depicted rural setting forms a contrast with the Mannerist elegance of the group of noblemen and valets.   A.C.

Dirk Vellert
Active between 1511 and 1544

40. *A Woman Bathing*

TECHNIQUE. Pen and brown ink. (28 x 12.5 cm.). Signed at lower left with the monogram: *DV*, with a five-point star.

PROVENANCE. Acquired by the Louvre during the Revolution. Inventory 18.804.

BIBLIOGRAPHY. M. Rooses, in *Onze Kunst*, 1902, pp. 169-170.
A. E. Popham, *Drawings of the Early Flemish School*, 1926, no. 56, repr.
A. J. J. Delen, *Teekeningen van Vlaamsche Meesters*, (1943), pp. 59-60, pl. XVIII, fig. 21.

Thanks to G. Glück, the true personality of Dirk Vellert, an engraver, draughtsman and stained-glass artist from Antwerp, was revealed in 1901 ("Beiträge zur Geschichte der Antwerpner Malerei im XVI. Jahrhundert," in *Jahrbuch der Kunsthistorischen Sämmlungen des Allerhöchsten Kaiserhauses*, vol. XXII). The artist left a great many pen and ink drawings in his broad, free style. They are mainly studies for stained glass windows, among which special mention should be made of the series of eighteen drawings for the *Apocalypse*, belonging to the Edmond de Rothschild Collection in the Louvre (Inventory 589–605 L.R.). It is not surprising that the influence of Dürer can usually be detected in these works; Vellert met with the master on three occasions, when the latter passed through Antwerp (September 1520, January and May 1521), and received the sequence of the *Apocalypse* as a gift.

An interesting comparison might be made between the present drawing, apparently the only known study after nature by Vellert, and Dürer's *Women Bathing* in Bremen; Vellert's drawing is an adaptation by one of Antwerp's finest talents of a theme imported from across the Rhine, until then rarely represented in the art of the Netherlands.   A.C.

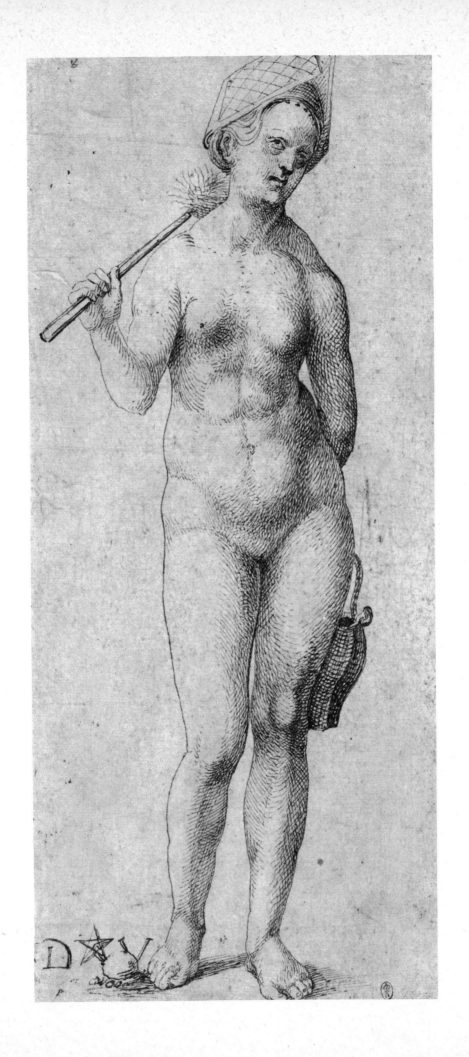

Stradanus

Jan van der Straeten

1523 - 1605

41. *The Tiger Hunt*

TECHNIQUE. Pen and brown ink, brown wash, heightened with white gouache. (18.5 x 26.1 cm.). Signed and dated in pen and ink at lower left: *Joans Stradanno Achademico di fiorenza 1596.*

PROVENANCE. E. Jabach; paraphs on verso of gilt bordered mount (Lugt 2959 and 2953) and the number: *deux cent douze*. Purchased for the Royal Collection in 1671.
Inventory 20.494.

The XVII century collector, E. Jabach, owned a series of sixteen compositions by Stradanus depicting hunting and fishing scenes and combats between men and animals. The present sheet was part of this group, and like several others it reappears in an engraved series by H. Collaert and Ph. Galle, entitled *Venationes Ferarum, Avium, Piscium, Pugnae Bestiarium et mutuae bestiarium* (pl. 16 of the series; Hollstein, vol. IV, nos. 173-188 and vol. VII, nos. 424-522). The drawings are extremely interesting and highly picturesque in subject; note, for example, the clever trap in the right foreground devised to lure the tigress into the cage. At the lower left an inscription with the date 1596, also appearing on two other sheets, *Men in Armor Fighting Bears* (Inventory 20.498) and *Elephants Carrying Palm Trees* (Inventory 20.499), marks a high point in the artist's career: his election as one of its first members to the Academy of Florence, founded in 1562.

When compared to Van Orley's *Hunting Scenes* (see no. 39), the drawings in this series, like certain tapestries designed by Stradanus for the Grand Duke Francesco of Tuscany which are now in the Palazzo Vecchio in Florence, may seem somewhat naive; nonetheless, they are the ingenious creations of a highly inventive mind.   A.C.

Joans stradanus
Achademie di fiore

Pieter Brueghel the Elder
About 1525/1530 - 1569

42. *Alpine Landscape*

TECHNIQUE. Pen and brown ink. (23.6 x 34.3 cm.). Dated in pen and ink at lower center: *1553*; inscribed below: *BRUEGHEL.*

PROVENANCE. P. Crozat; sale, Paris, 1741, no. 904(?). P. J. Mariette; stamp at lower left (Lugt 1852) and mounted with: *PETRUS BREUGHEL Senior* inscribed in a cartouche; sale, 1775, part of lot no. 840. Bought at this sale for the Royal Collection.
Inventory 19.728.

BIBLIOGRAPHY. K. Tolnay, *Die Zeichnungen Pieter Bruegels*, Munich, 1925, pp. 5, 6, 80, no. 8, repr.
Ch. de Tolnay, "Bruegel et l'Italie," in *Les Arts plastiques*, August 2, 1951, p. 122, repr. detail fig. 65.
Ch. de Tolnay, *The Drawings of Pieter Bruegel the Elder*, London, 1952, pp. 44, 57, no. 10, pl. 6.
L. Münz, *The Drawings of Bruegel*, London, 1961, no. 5, pl. 5.
Le Cabinet d'un grand amateur, P. J. Mariette, Exhibition Catalogue, Paris, Louvre, 1967, no. 156, repr.

As the date indicates, this drawing is among the first landscapes executed by Brueghel during his stay in Italy between 1552 and 1554. In the course of his travels the artist sought out picturesque sites for drawings executed in view of engravings, and like Dürer (see no. 4), sketched numerous landscapes, now in the Louvre, the British Museum, and the Liechtenstein Collection (Tolnay, 1952, nos. 7-9). These works reveal the deep impression made by the mountainous regions through which he passed, while the free treatment of space, light and shadow reflects the influence of the Venetian landscape painters working in the entourage of Titian. The Alpine landscape represented here, particularly admired by Mariette when he catalogued the Crozat Collection, is expressive of the artist's vision in the importance given to nature and the epic grandeur of the gigantic mountain overlooking the plain, contrasting with the houses and figures of reduced proportions. As a cosmic vision of nature, it is reminiscent of certain works by Patinir; however, the sincere and profound observation is highly personal, marking Brueghel as one of the great landscape artists of his century. The Louvre has a second Alpine landscape, also dated 1533, which belonged to Mariette (Inventory 19.727).   A.C.

Martin de Vos
1532 - 1603

43. *Decorative Project*

TECHNIQUE. Pen and brown ink, brown and gray wash, heightened with blue and white watercolor. (34.7 x 29 cm.). Signed and dated in pen and ink at lower left: *M D VOS F 1588*.

PROVENANCE. P. J. Mariette; stamp at lower right (Lugt 1852) and mounted with: *MARTINUS DE VOS* inscribed in a cartouche; sale, Paris, 1775, no. 1060. Bought at this sale for the Royal Collection. Inventory 20.592.

BIBLIOGRAPHY. W. Wegner, "Drawings by Pozzoserrato," in *Master Drawings*, 1963, I, no. 4, p. 30.
Le Seizième Siècle européen. Dessins du Louvre, Exhibition Catalogue, Paris, Louvre, 1965, no. 250, pl. LXVI.

Martin de Vos, who first studied under his father, Peter de Vos, and later under Frans Floris, became, after the latter's death, the most fashionable painter in Antwerp. Successfully combining the clever eclecticism of Floris and the brilliance of Venetian colors, he emerges as the direct forerunner of the Baroque school in Antwerp. According to the catalogue of the Mariette sale, the present drawing is probably a tapestry project for the door curtain of an apartment, though W. Wegner thinks it more likely the design for the frontispiece of a book. A beautiful example of Flemish decorative art, it is particularly interesting for the different influences seen in juxtaposition. The arrangement of the rich medley of trophies adorning the border recalls certain decorations by Floris, while the small decorative landscape is clearly inspired by a view of Venice. This is not surprising, since Martin de Vos lived from 1548-1558 in Italy, working in Rome in the atmosphere of the Mannerist circles and also in Venice, where his activity as a student and collaborator of Tintoretto was mainly devoted to landscapes.   A.C.

Denis Calvaert

About 1540 - 1619

44. *The Mystic Marriage of Saint Catherine*

TECHNIQUE. Pen and brown ink, brown wash, heightened with white. (26.7 x 20.3 cm.).

PROVENANCE. Alfonso III d'Este, Duke of Modena; stamp on verso (Lugt 112). Francesco II, Duke of Modena; stamp on verso (Lugt 1893). Acquired by the Louvre in 1797.
Inventory 19.836.

BIBLIOGRAPHY. S. Bergmans, "Denis Calvart peintre anversois, fondateur de l'Ecole bolonaise du XVIe siècle," in *Revue d' Art*, LXV, 1928, pp. 172-173, pl. 165.
S. Bergmans, "Catalogue critique des œuvres du peintre Calvart," in *Mémoires de l'Académie Royale de Belgique*, IV, Brussels, 1931, p. 23.
S. Bergmans, "Denis Calvart, peintre anversois, et fondateur de l'Ecole bolonaise," in *Mémoires de l' Académie Royale de Belgique*, IV, Brussels, 1934, pp. 49-50.
Le Seizième Siècle européen. Dessins du Louvre, Exhibition Catalogue, Paris, Louvre, 1965, no. 196, pl. L.

Simone Bergmans' discovery of a painting of this subject, signed and dated 1590, which is now in the Capitol in Rome, led to a more precise identification of the present drawing (*Le Siècle de Bruegel*, Exhibition Catalogue, Brussels, 1963, no. 64, fig. 253). The final work differs in certain respects from this study: the landscape is slightly modified and the composition less dense; the angels bearing the crown, Saint Joseph and the figures seen behind the Virgin have been suppressed.

As the date indicates, this drawing, often exhibited throughout the XIX century, belongs to Calvaert's latest and best period. The Italian influence apparent here is explained by the fact that the artist, who arrived in Italy around 1562, frequently copied the Italian masters and was especially drawn to the painters of the Parma school. Nonetheless, the way in which he lends the intimate and familiar charm of a genre study to a religious subject is characteristic of Flemish art.

Calvaert founded an academy in Bologna which preceded that of the Carracci and was to become widely celebrated during his lifetime; among its students were such well-known artists as Guido Reni, Domenichino, Albani, and Guercino.   A.C.

Joris Hoefnagel
1542 - 1600

and

Jacob Hoefnagel
1575 - 1630

45. *Diana and Actaeon*

The scene is framed with a garland of flowers and insects. At the center of lateral borders is a vase holding a white tulip.

TECHNIQUE. Watercolor, heightened with gold, on vellum. (22 x 33.9 cm.). Signed and dated at the center and below the scene: *Georgius Houfnaglius Pa. and Jacobus Fi. FF Anno MCCCCCXCVII.* Latin texts in gold lettering in cartouches, against a blue background at upper center and a black background at lower center.

PROVENANCE. Sale, Paris, December 16, 1942, no. 41, pl. III. In trust with the Louvre.

BIBLIOGRAPHY. *Le Seizième Siècle européen. Dessins du Louvre*, Exhibition Catalogue, Paris, Louvre, 1965, no. 171, pl. XLII.

A student of Hans Bol renowned for his paintings of flowers, Joris Hoefnagel was one of the representative artists from Antwerp's commercial and humanist circles. In addition to being a painter, he was a jeweler, poet and cartographer as well as a collector of drawings; he worked for the Duke of Bavaria and the Emperor Rudolph II in Vienna and in Prague, where his son Jacob carried on the style developed by his father. He executed illuminations for albums representing plants and flowers, as well as a few isolated miniatures similar to the one reproduced; examples of the miniatures can be seen in the Royal Library in Brussels (M. L. Hairs, *Les Peintres flamands de fleurs au XVIIe siècle*, Paris-Brussels, 1955, pp. 13, 223).

Poetic and at the same time realistic, this type of landscape, already found in the works of Hans Bol (see no. 71), is in the tradition of XV century illuminations; however, the analytic, almost scientific description of the plants and insects decorating the border is an original contribution of the artist, which makes him a forerunner of a style destined to become extremely popular in the Netherlands, from the time of Brueghel, called "Velvet." It seems likely, therefore, that the mythological scene in the present watercolor was executed by Jacob, the son, and the decorative border by his father.   A.C.

VENATOR CASSES, ET CASSES FEDIT AMATOR,
QVOS SÆPE INCASSVM TENDIT VTERQ; TAME.
EX ÆQVO FLVVIAS, ET VENTOS SPERNIT VTERQ;,
DAMNOSOS NVTRIT STVLTVS VTERQ;VE CANES.

ATTAMEN HOC DISTAT QVOD CV FERA STERNITVR ALER
PRÆMIA SOLLICITI IVSTA LABORVM HABET.
TVM DEMVM VERO INFELIX SVPERATVR AMATOR,
CVM SIMILIS VICTÆ PRÆDA SVPINA IACET.

Bartholomeus Spranger

1546 - 1611

46. *Judith Giving the Head of Holophernes to a Servant*

TECHNIQUE. Pen and brown ink, brown wash, heightened with white, on prepared paper. (32.1 x 21.4 cm.). Inscribed in pen and ink at lower right: *Spranger* $^{1}/_{12}f$.

PROVENANCE. Acquired by the Louvre before 1827.
Inventory 20.474.

BIBLIOGRAPHY. A. Niederstein, "Das graphische Werk des Bartholomaeüs Spranger," in *Repertorium für Kunstwissenschaft*, 52, 1931, pp. 16-17, 20, fig. 8, p. 17.
O. Benesch, *The Art of the Renaissance in Northern Europe*, Cambridge, Mass., 1947, p. 133.
K. Oberhuber, *Die Stilistische Entwicklung im Werk Bartolomaeüs Spranger*, Vienna, 1958, p. 196, Cat. no. 243 (thesis).
Le Seizième Siècle europèen. Dessins du Louvre, Exhibition Catalogue, Paris, Louvre, 1965, no. 172, pl. LXVI.

The highly supple and elegant delineation of these two female figures recalls the fact that Spranger, during his stay in Italy, between 1566 and 1575, was especially attracted by the art of the Parma school and influenced by both Roman and Tuscan Mannerism, before becoming himself one of the most important masters of international Mannerism at the end of the XVI century. In his thesis, K. Oberhuber contends that this drawing belongs among the works executed by the artist between 1606-1607, during his last period in Prague, where he had been living since 1581; he suggests that it may have been part of a lost series of drawings illustrating the power of women. However, A. Niederstein favors an earlier date; in his opinion the drawing stylistically resembles Spranger's work during the years 1590–1598, at which time the court of Rudolph II, under the dual influence of Spranger and Heintz, developed a somewhat acid form of preciosity very different from all its Italian antecedents (Parmigianino, Anselmi). In view of the fact that in his later works Spranger tended to prefer fuller faces and forms to the elongated female type represented here, we are also inclined to favor the earlier date.

A drawing of the same subject was classified in Spranger's name in the Paignon-Dijonval Collection (Paris, 1810, Catalogue, no. 1253, p. 62).   A.C.

Pietro Candido
Pieter de Witte
1548(?) - 1628

47. *The Descent from the Cross*

TECHNIQUE. Pen and brown ink over traces of black chalk, brown wash, heightened with white, on gray-green paper. (54 x 40.8 cm.). Squared up in red chalk. Inscribed in pen and ink at lower left: *Dipinto da me Pietro Candido per uno altare alla badia di S. Giusto poco fuora di Volterra questo e il secondo altare di mio mano in detta chiesa*; and on verso: *Petrus Candidu né à Bruge en 1548. Il est mort en Italie ou* (il) *a toujours demeuré.*

PROVENANCE. P. J. Mariette; stamp at lower right and left (Lugt 1852) and mounted with: *PETRUS CANDIDUS BELGA* inscribed in a cartouche; sale, Paris, 1775, no. 273. Acquired by the Louvre during the Revolution; unidentified paraph on verso.
Inventory 19.853.

BIBLIOGRAPHY. N. Steinbart, "Pieter Candido in Italien," in *Jahrbuch der Königlich preussischen Kunstsammlungen*, 1937, p. 71, fig. 6.
Le Seizième Siècle européen. Dessins du Louvre, Exhibition Catalogue, Paris, Louvre, 1965, no. 198, pl. LI.

As the inscription indicates, this is a preparatory study for a painting executed by Pietro Candido for the Abbey of Saint Just near Volterra. Both this painting and a *Nativity* painted in 1580 for the abbey, which was destroyed in 1895, are now in the Pinacoteca in Volterra.

From the hand of an artist who spent many years of his life in Rome and Florence (1570–1586) before working in Munich in the service of William V, this beautiful composition, dated about 1580–1585 by K. Steinbart, is a significant indication of the artistic exchange between Italy and Northern Europe at the end of the XVI century. Another drawing representing the same subject, with certain differences in the arrangement of the scene, bears an old attribution to Martin de Vos, although A. E. Popham believes it to be the work of Pietro Candido (A. E. Popham, *Catalogue by Dutch and Flemish Artists Preserved in the British Museum. XV and XVI Centuries*, 1932, p. 97, no. 1, repr. pl. LXXVIII). The Prado also has a study for a *Pietà* by this artist which, like the present drawing, formerly belonged to Mariette.   A.C.

Frans Pourbus the Younger

1569 - 1622

48. *Magistrates Paying Homage to the Young Louis XIII*

TECHNIQUE. Pen and brown ink, brown wash, heightened with white, traces of black chalk. (22 x 19.3 cm.).

PROVENANCE. P. J. Mariette; stamp at lower right (Lugt 1852) and mount partially trimmed, with: *FRANCISCUS POURBUS* inscribed in a cartouche; above: *PRAEFECTUR AEDILES LUDOVICUM XIII. DE NUPTIIS GRATULANTUR: PRAECOGITATIO TABULAE IN BASILICA PACIS, DEPICTAE ANNO 1618;.* sale, Paris, 1775, no. 1319. Bought at this sale for the Royal Collection.
Inventory 20.170.

BIBLIOGRAPHY. G. Brière, M. Dumoulin and P. Jarry, *Les Tableaux de l'Hôtel de Ville de Paris*, 1937, p. 14.
Lugt, *Flamands*, 1949, vol. II, no. 990, pl. VII.
J. Wilhelm, "Pourbus peintre de la municipalité parisienne," in *Arts de France*, 1963, pp. 114-123, repr. p. 115 and details pp. 116-117.
Le Cabinet d' un grand amateur, P. J. Mariette, Exhibition Catalogue, Paris, Louvre, 1967, no. 191.

Frans Pourbus the Younger, son of Frans Pourbus the Elder, worked for the Duke of Gonzaga in Mantua before coming to Paris in 1609 at the request of Marie de Medicis. Possessing a ready and substantial talent, he rapidly became the official court portraitist, who is now best known for his isolated drawn or painted portraits. Here, the Louvre claims one of his rare compositional projects—a study for one of the paintings that adorned the Great Hall of the Hôtel-de-Ville—dating from the artist's period in Paris and connected with a decorative ensemble greatly admired by his contemporaries.

The subject of the present composition has been diversely interpreted. Originally it was believed to be a first idea for the painting which shows the city magistrates come to congratulate the young King Louis XIII on the occasion of his marriage in 1615 (Basan, Catalogue, Mariette Sale). However, J. Wilhelm's studies have shown that the ceremony depicted here could not have taken place before 1616; the work is therefore more probably a project for one of the large paintings commissioned about 1618 by another provostship.   A.C.

Paul Bril

1554 - 1626

49. *Mountainous Landscape with a Hermit*

TECHNIQUE. Pen and brown ink, brown wash, heightened with blue. (19.7 x 27.2 cm.).

PROVENANCE. E. Jabach; paraph at lower left (Lugt 2961). Purchased for the Royal Collection in 1671.
Inventory 19.779.

BIBLIOGRAPHY. A. Mayer, *Das Leben und die Werke der Brüder Matthaus und Paul Bril*, Leipzig, 1910, p. 79, no. 7.
Lugt, *Flamands*, 1949, vol. I, no. 397, pl. XXIX.

Paul Bril arrived in Rome in 1580, shortly after his brother, Matthew. Like Elsheimer, he is one of the painters who most contributed to a renewal of the art of the landscape in Italy. His evolution towards an increasingly free and natural style can be traced in the numerous drawings, mostly pen and ink sketches frequently heightened with wash and watercolor, which are now in the Louvre.

A. Meyer dates the present composition about 1605 ; F. Lugt, on the other hand, believes it may have been executed immediately after a series of frescos representing figures of saints in landscape backgrounds, which were painted in 1599 for the Santa Cecilia Church in Rome. While springing from the Flemish tradition, the drawing also reflects Bril's sensitivity to the Italian influence. The decorative aspect of the landscape and its luminosity give evidence of the changes in his conception between 1590–1600, when the traditional intimate landscape of the Netherlands is fused in his work with the composed landscape characteristic of the Bolognese school.

An engraving of this drawing by E. Sadeler served as the model for a painting by P. Stevens which is now in the Brunswick Museum. The same landscape was engraved by Caylus in the XVIII century for a collection of prints executed after drawings from the Royal Collection (1729, pl. 213).   A.C.

Peter Paul Rubens

1577 - 1640

50. *A Gentleman in Armor on Horseback*

TECHNIQUE. Pen and brown ink, brown wash over traces of black chalk. (29.8 x 21.6 cm.). Inscribed in pencil at lower center: *Rubens*. The horseman's head is drawn on an added piece of paper.

PROVENANCE. E. Jabach; paraph (Lugt 1964). Purchased for the Royal Collection in 1671; at lower approximate left, paraph by R. de Cotte (Lugt 1961). Inventory 20.185.

BIBLIOGRAPHY. M. Rooses, *L'Œuvre de P. P. Rubens*, Antwerp, vol. V, 1892, no. 1503.
G. Glück, and F. M. Haberditzl, *Die Handzeichnungen von Peter Paul Rubens*, Berlin, 1928, no. 46, repr.
Lugt, *Flamands*, 1949, vol. II, no. 1018, pl. XIX.
J. S. Held, *Rubens Drawings*, London, 1959, I, no. 71; repr. II, fig. 83.
L. Burchard and R. A. d'Hulst, *Rubens Drawings*, Brussels, 1963, vol. I, no. 30; repr. vol. II, fig. 30.

Listed in old inventories as a portrait of Charles V, this drawing was correctly identified by Glück who recognized it as a study for the *Equestrian Portrait of the Duke of Lerma*, a painting executed by Rubens on the occasion of his meeting with Philip III's all powerful minister. The painting now belongs to the Countess Viuda de Gavia (repr. A. Rosenberg, *P. P. Rubens. Des Meisters Gemälde*, Stuttgart-Leipzig, 1906, p. 5). The features as depicted here are not those of the duke, and some scholars have suggested that one of the duke's squires may have served as the model.

For a youthful work, this first equestrian portrait displays a remarkable sureness, anticipating some of the artist's later battle and hunting scenes. As A. L. Mayer has pointed out (*El Greco*, Berlin-Leipzig, 1931, p. 104), the portrait may have been suggested by El Greco's *Saint Martin* (National Gallery, Washington); but whatever the source of inspiration, Rubens has introduced here a new pattern into equestrian portraiture—the plastic image of a horseman, previously reserved for religious or mythological compositions.

The collection of the Grand Duke of Saxe-Weimar-Eisenach formerly contained a second and larger drawing showing the same composition (repr. Glück-Haberditzl, fig. 47); though certain historians have questioned its authenticity, Held and Burchard both contend that it is by Rubens.   A.C.

Peter Paul Rubens
1577 - 1640

51. *Augustus and the Sibyl, after Pordenone*

TECHNIQUE. Watercolor over traces of black and red chalk. (29.7 x 33.4 cm.). Inscribed in pen and ink at upper left on added sheet of paper: *In concavo hoc depictum est | e lateribus utrinq* (ne) *Templum Pacis | quod procul visentibus integrum stare videtur | appropinquantibus vero et hapsidem subeuntibus | corruere ac plane dissolvi | pinxit Pordenone Tarvisii.* Band 2.2 cm. in width pasted the length of lower border.

PROVENANCE. P. J. Mariette; stamp at lower right (Lugt 1852) and mounted with: *PET. PAUL RUBENS AD PICTUR PORDENONE* inscribed in a cartouche. His de la Salle; stamp at lower left (Lugt 1333); given to the Louvre in 1878.
Inventory RF 702.

BIBLIOGRAPHY. M. Rooses, *L'Œuvre de P. P. Rubens*, Antwerp, vol. V, 1892, p. 201, no. 1383, pl. 397.
G. Glück and F. M. Haberditzl, *Die Handzeichnungen von Peter Paul Rubens*, Berlin, 1928, no. 1, repr.
Lugt, *Flamands*, 1949, vol. II, no. 1065, pl. XLIII.
L. Burchard and R. A. d'Hulst, *Rubens Drawings*, Brussels, 1963, vol. I, cited under no. 24.
Le Cabinet d'un grand amateur. P. J. Mariette, Exhibition Catalogue, Paris, Louvre, 1967, no. 195.

The Louvre has an exceptionally rich collection of studies and copies made by Rubens after Classical artists and Renaissance masters, many of which came from the Jabach Collection. This large watercolor, which belonged to Mariette, is the artist's interpretation of a fresco by Pordenone decorating one of the recesses in the Malchiostro Chapel of San Nicolò in Treviso (repr. G. Fiocco, *Giovanni Antonio Pordenone*, Padua, 1943, fig. 77). According to Burchard and D'Hulst, the subject of the fresco appears to be *Augustus and the Sibyl* and not, as previously indicated, *Saint Liberalis and an Angel.*

It is likely that Rubens executed this study early in his stay in Italy; stylistically it lacks the full vigor of his later drawings, but the artist's originality is already expressed in the breadth of the two figures. A second study after Pordenone, which also belonged to Mariette and is now in the collection of Count Seilern, represents the figure of God, taken from the fresco that previously adorned the cupola of the Malchiostro Chapel. Classified by Mariette among drawings by Pordenone, the latter sheet was restored to Rubens by A. E. Popham (*Old Master Drawings*, December 1933, p. 43).   A. C.

Peter Paul Rubens

1577 - 1640

52. *The Baptism of Christ*

TECHNIQUE. Black chalk. Squared up in black chalk. (48.6 x 76.7 cm.). A few pieces of paper added after squaring up (notably in the foliage of the main tree and near left hip of a young man seated at center).

PROVENANCE. E. Jabach; paraphs on verso of gilt bordered mount (Lugt 2959 and 2953). Purchased for the Royal Collection in 1671. Inventory 20.187.

BIBLIOGRAPHY. M. Rooses, *L'Œuvre de P. P. Rubens*, Antwerp, vol. II, 1885, p. 5; vol. V, 1892, no. 1343, pl. 384.
G. Glück, F. M. Haberditzl, *Die Handzeichnungen von Peter Paul Rubens*, Berlin, 1928, no. 50, repr.
Lugt, *Flamands*, 1949, vol. II, no. 1009, pl. XIV.
J. S. Held, *Rubens, Selected Drawings*, London, 1959, vol. I, no. 11; repr. vol. II, fig. 12.
L. Burchard and R. A. d'Hulst, *Rubens Drawings*, Brussels, 1963, vol. I, no. 29; repr. vol. II, fig. 29.

The attribution of this drawing to Van Dyck in the Jabach inventory was questioned by M. Rooses; however, E. Michel was the first to assign it definitely to Rubens, in his book on the artist published in 1900. Rubens' drawn projects for painted compositions were rarely executed with such precision, hence the exceptional interest of the present study for one of three paintings commissioned by the Duke of Gonzaga for the Santa Trinità Church in Mantua, which were completed in May of 1605. Certain variations in the painting, now in Antwerp (repr. A. Rosenberg, *P. P. Rubens. Des Meisters Gemälde*, Stuttgart-Leipzig, 1906, p. 22) should be noted, in particular the introduction of two cherubs above the Holy Ghost, the modified gesture of Saint John, and the suppression of the seated figure of a young man at the center of the drawing.

This large drawing, the most important to come down to us from the artist's early period, is reminiscent of both Classical art —in the pose of the seated young man, for example—and the art of the Renaissance—the right part of the composition, in particular, is clearly inspired by Michelangelo. Yet it is unmistakably Rubens, already displaying some of the basic traits of his style: freedom of composition, a sure and vigorous line, and figures of monumental breadth.   A. C.

Peter Paul Rubens

1577 - 1640

53. *Study of a Male Nude Lifting a Heavy Object*

TECHNIQUE. Black chalk, heightened with white. (43 x 54.8 cm.). Inscribed in black chalk at upper right near the elbow: *per lazaro;* at lower left, in another hand: *P. P. Rubens*, and, in pen and ink at lower right the number: *30*.

PROVENANCE. The Royal Collection.
Inventory 20.218.

BIBLIOGRAPHY. G. Glück, F. M. Haberditzl, *Die Handzeichnungen von Peter Paul Rubens*, Berlin, 1928, no. 92, repr.
Lugt, *Flamands*, 1949, vol. II, no. 1030, pl. XXVIII.
De Tekeningen van P. P. Rubens, Exhibition Catalogue, Antwerp, 1956, no. 59, pl. XXII.
L. Burchard and R. A. d'Hulst, *Rubens Drawings*, Brussels, 1963, vol. I, no. 91; repr. vol. II, fig. 91.

The present drawing is a study after nature for the figure of the man seen setting down a vase in the right foreground of the *Meeting of Abraham and Melchizedek*, a painting in the Caen Museum generally dated about 1615 (repr. R. Oldenbourg and A. Rosenberg, *P. P. Rubens. Des Meisters Gemälde*, Stuttgart-Berlin, 1921, p. 110, 4th ed.). The artist repeats here, with certain variations, the attitude of one of the figures in the *Adoration of the Magi*, a painting in the Prado which was executed about 1610 (repr. R. Oldenbourg and A. Rosenberg, p. 26). A direct study for the Prado painting, in the same technique and after the same model as the Louvre drawing, is in the Boymans Museum in Rotterdam (repr. Burchard-D'Hulst, fig. 92).

Stylistically very similar, the two drawings show the same skillful foreshortening, vigorous modeling and sculptural forms; it is possible that both were executed by Rubens while he was working on the Prado *Adoration of the Magi*, in which case he chose the attitude of the figure studied in the Boymans drawing for the latter and used the present drawing, a few years later, for the canvas in the Caen Museum. A. C.

Peter Paul Rubens

1577 - 1640

54. *Study of Trees*

TECHNIQUE. Black chalk, contours reworked in pen and brown ink by the artist. (58.2 x 48.9 cm.). Numbered in pen and ink at lower right: *3*.

PROVENANCE. Acquired by the Louvre during the Revolution. Inventory 20.212.

BIBLIOGRAPHY. M. Rooses, *L'Œuvre de P. P. Rubens*, Antwerp, vol. V, 1892, p. 301, no. 1591, pl. 430.
E. Michel, *Rubens, sa vie, son œuvre et son temps*, Paris, 1900, p. 254, pl. XIX, opp. p. 252.
Lugt, *Flamands*, 1949, vol. II, no. 1034, pl. XXXI.
J. S. Held, *Rubens Drawings*, London, 1959, vol. I, no. 131; repr. vol. II, fig. 140.
L. Burchard and R. A. d'Hulst, *Rubens Drawings*, Brussels, 1963, vol. I, no. 104; repr. vol. II, fig. 104.

This remarkably dynamic drawing, based on extremely precise observation, is, of all the trees and plants sketched by Rubens, unanimously considered his most beautiful study after nature. E. Michel was the first to point out that the motif of trees and undergrowth is repeated with certain variations at the extreme left of the *Boar Hunt*, a painting in the Dresden Museum dated about 1616 (repr. A. Rosenberg, *P. P. Rubens. Des Meisters Gemälde*, Stuttgart-Leipzig, 1906, p. 214). The collection of the Duke of Devonshire in Chatsworth contains a lightly colored black chalk sketch of the tree shown here, studied in breadth, which Rubens used about ten years later in his *Landscape with Ulysses and Nausicaä* (Pitti Palace, repr. Rosenberg, p. 354). A second study in the Chatsworth Collection, representing a branch and undergrowth, can also be connected with the Louvre drawing (repr. Burchard-D'Hulst, vol. II, no. 105), while a large drawing in the Albertina repeats the composition of the present sheet, with human and animal figures added; the latter work has been alternately attributed to Rubens and Soutman. These various studies, at once robust, true to nature and heroic, are brilliant illustrations of Rubens' qualities as a landscape artist.   A. C.

Peter Paul Rubens
1577 - 1640

55. *Portrait of Marie de Medicis*

TECHNIQUE. Black and red chalk, heightened with white. (35.5 x 27.7 cm.). Inscribed in pen and ink at upper right: *Rubens*; at lower left: *Reyne mere*; and at lower right, the number: *81*. A strip of paper has been pasted vertically along the edge of the right border of the main sheet.

PROVENANCE. P. Crozat; sale, Paris, 1741, part of lot no. 843. Agor. Count C. G. Tessin. Louisa Ulrica, Queen of Sweden. Princess Sophia Albertina. Count G. Stenbock (inscriptions on verso of the drawing, probably in the hand of Count Nils Barck). Count Nils Barck; stamp at lower left (Lugt 1959). Purchased by the Louvre in 1853.
Inventory 20.224.

BIBLIOGRAPHY: M. Rooses, *L'Œuvre de P. P. Rubens*, Antwerp, vol. V, 1892, p. 268, no. 1014, pl. 422.
G. Glück, F. M. Haberditzl, *Die Handzeichnungen von Peter Paul Rubens*, Berlin, 1928, no. 150, repr.
Lugt, *Flamands*, 1949, vol. II, no. 1020, pl. XXI.
Les plus beaux Dessins du Louvre, Exhibition Catalogue, Paris, Louvre, 1962, no. 44.

In 1622, at the request of Marie de Medicis, whose portrait he had recently painted (Prado), Rubens began work on the decoration of one of the large galleries of the new Luxembourg Palace. The artist executed fifteen panels presenting an *Apologia for Marie de Medicis and Her Government*, and in May of 1625, on the occasion of the betrothal of Henriette of France to the Prince of Wales, the gallery was inaugurated. The paintings remained in place until 1778, when they were exhibited in the Senate; in 1815, they were removed to the Louvre where they can still be seen.

Rubens was the first painter from the Netherlands to receive a commission for a decorative ensemble of such scope, and he displayed inexhaustible imagination in the accomplishment of his task. The present drawing is a study for the figure of Marie de Medicis in the composition depicting the *Felicity of the Regency*, in which the queen is seen seated, holding the scepter and the scales of Justice (repr. A. Rosenberg, *P. P. Rubens. Des Meisters Gemälde*, Stuttgart-Leipzig, 1905, p. 257). Apart from its obvious iconographical interest, this study for an official portrait reveals certain traits—notably the frank treatment of the face and the direct impression of life—which are characteristic of Rubens' portraiture. Two additional portraits of Marie de Medicis, also related to the Luxembourg cycle, are now in the Victoria and Albert Museum and the Albertina (repr. Glück-Haberditzl, figs. 151-152).   A. C.

Peter Paul Rubens

1577 - 1640

56. *Minerva and Hercules Repelling Mars*

TECHNIQUE. Oil diluted with turpentine over a black chalk sketch. (37 x 53.9 cm.).

PROVENANCE. E. Jabach; paraph (Lugt 1961). Purchased for the Royal Collection in 1671 ; at lower left, paraph of R. de Cotte (Lugt 1964). Inventory 20.183.

BIBLIOGRAPHY. M. Rooses, *L'Œuvre de P. P. Rubens*, Antwerp, vol. IV, 1890, under the no. 826; vol. V, 1892, no. 1475.
G. Glück, F. M. Haberditzl, *Die Handzeichnungen von Peter Paul Rubens*, Berlin, 1928, no. 182, repr.
Lugt, *Flamands*, 1949, vol. II, no. 1014, pl. XVI.
De Tekeningen van P. P. Rubens, Exhibition Catalogue, Antwerp, 1956, no. 115, pl. XLVIII.
L. Burchard and R. A. d'Hulst, *Rubens Drawings*, Brussels, 1963, vol. I, no. 169; repr. vol. II, fig. 169.

After Rubens had played an active role in the negotiations between Spain and England, the opposition of war and peace became one of his favorite themes and the subject of many allegorical compositions. The present drawing, one of the most significant in this respect, can be related to several paintings representing *Minerva Defending Peace*, notably those in the London National Gallery and the Munich Pinakothek (repr. A. Rosenberg, *P. P. Rubens. Des Meisters Gemälde*, Stuttgart-Leipzig, 1906, pp. 297, 311). J. S. Held *(Rubens Drawings*, London, 1959, I, no. 66) relates it more specifically to the large *Allegory of War* in the Pitti Palace (repr. Rosenberg, p. 434), noting that in the latter work Rubens manifests a certain pessimism; in the encounter between Minerva, symbol of Peace, and Mars, god of War, the struggle appears to be turning in favor of the god.

This ardently dynamic and freely executed drawing can be dated about 1630-1635 ; typically Baroque in spirit, it is treated with a bold freedom characteristic of Rubens' sketches (for example, the painted sketches for the decoration of the *Torre de la Parada*, which are now in Brussels). In the Boymans Museum there is a drawing in the same technique representing the central group of figures.   A. C.

Peter Paul Rubens

1577 - 1640

57. *Young Woman Holding a Fan*

TECHNIQUE. Black and red chalk, heightened with white, with a few traces of brush and China ink. (53.6 x 34.8 cm.).

PROVENANCE. J. Barnard; later inscribed on verso with the number: *797* (Lugt 1420). Acquired by the Louvre during the Revolution. Inventory 20.196.

BIBLIOGRAPHY. M. Rooses, *L'Œuvre de P. P. Rubens*, Antwerp, vol. IV, 1890, p. 65. under the no. 835; vol. V, 1892, p. 248, no. 1447, pl. 416.
G. Glück, F. M. Haberditzl, *Die Handzeichnungen von Peter Paul Rubens*, Berlin, 1928, no. 204, repr.
Lugt, *Flamands*, 1949, vol. II, no. 1023, pl. XXIII.
J. S. Held, *Rubens Drawings*, London, 1959, vol. I, no. 118; repr. vol. II, fig. 130.
L. Burchard and R. A. d'Hulst, *Rubens Drawings*, Brussels, 1963, vol. I, no. 182; repr. vol. II, fig. 182.

This is a study for the somewhat modified figure of the young woman seen at the foot of a fountain at the right in the painting known as the *Garden of Love*, or a *Gallant Conversation*, which is now in the Prado (repr. A. Rosenberg, *P. P. Rubens. Des Meisters Gemälde*, Stuttgart-Leipzig, 1906, p. 388). Judging from the exceptionally large number of known preliminary works relating to it, Rubens appears to have executed the painting with unusual care; in addition to two large composition sketches in the Metropolitan Museum in New York (repr. Held, II, figs. 162-163), there is a carefully worked drawing for almost every main figure. A second Louvre study is connected with the young woman seen stooping at the foot of the steps at left in the final composition (Inventory 20.194).

These broad and monumental drawings were executed between 1630-1633, at a time when Rubens was evolving towards a more intimate lyricism; stylistically evoking a world of elegance and opulence, they are a prelude to the *Fêtes Galantes* of Watteau. Helena Fourment, whom Rubens married on December 6, 1630, probably served as the model for the present study.   A. C.

Peter Paul Rubens

1577 - 1640

58. *Head of a Little Girl*

TECHNIQUE. Black and red chalk, heightened with white, contours reworked by the artist in pen and brown ink. (22.3 x 19.5 cm.).

PROVENANCE. Count Nils Barck; stamp at lower center (Lugt 1959). His de la Salle; stamp at lower left (Lugt 1333). Given to the Louvre in 1878. Inventory RF 700.

BIBLIOGRAPHY. Lugt, *Flamands*, 1949, vol. II, no. 1022, pl. XX.

Attempts have often been made to identify this mischievous little girl with one of Rubens' children by his second marriage, with Helena Fourment—possibly Claire-Jeanne, born in 1632, or Isabella-Helena, born in 1635. However, not enough is known of the two children to establish a comparison justifying this hypothesis.

Among Rubens scholars, F. Lugt is the only one to have given special attention to this charming and lively sketch, which stylistically resembles various other studies of the same type, notably the *Portrait of Robin*, the Earl of Arundel's dwarf, which is now in Stockholm (repr. J. S. Held, *Rubens Drawings*, London, 1959, vol. II, fig. 113). Rubens' portraits of children are without doubt among his most sensitive works, executed with all the tenderness of a deeply contented father. The playful expression of this little girl is an especially appealing illustration of his understanding of a child's nature.   A. C.

Peter Paul Rubens

1577 - 1640

59. *Self-Portrait*

TECHNIQUE. Black chalk, heightened with white. (46 x 28.5 cm.). Verso: figures rapidly sketched in pen and ink are visible through the effect of the paper's transparency.

PROVENANCE. J. Richardson, Senior; stamp at lower right (Lugt 2184). Th. Hudson. J. Barnard; later inscribed on verso with the number: *1066* (Lugt 1420). Acquired by the Louvre during the Revolution. Inventory 20.195.

BIBLIOGRAPHY. M. Rooses, *L'Œuvre de P. P. Rubens*, Antwerp, vol. V, 1892, pp. 276-277, no. 1530.
G. Glück, F. M. Haberditzl, *Die Handzeichnungen von Peter Paul Rubens*, Berlin, 1928, no. 235, repr.
Lugt, *Flamands*, 1949, vol. II, no. 1017, pl. XVIII.
J. S. Held, *Rubens Drawings*, London, 1959, vol. I, no. 123; repr. vol. II, fig. 126.
L. Burchard and R. A. d'Hulst, *Rubens Drawings*, Brussels, 1963, vol. I, no. 202; repr. vol. II, fig. 202.

Engraved in 1768 by Simon Watts and published in a work by C. Rogers, *Collection of Prints in Imitation of Drawings*, II, 1778, p. 211, this drawing is a study for the *Self Portrait* in the Vienna Museum (repr. A. Rosenberg, *P. P. Rubens. Des Meisters Gemälde*, Stuttgart-Leipzig, 1906, p. 437), one of the artist's late paintings. The final composition differs somewhat from the present work: the hat is slightly modified; a column in the background at the left and a sword handle have been introduced.

While equally famous, the drawing is perhaps more natural than the painting. It is a strikingly moving portrait in which the noble expression of the eyes contrasts with the look of deep weariness on the face. This and a slightly later *Self-Portrait* now in Windsor (repr. Held, II, fig. 139), are unquestionably the most poignant images of Rubens and the most intensely revealing of his great intelligence and lucid observation. In the British Museum there is a copy of the Louvre study, executed in the same technique and coming from the Paignon-Dijonval, the Marquis Morel de Vindé, and the Sir Thomas Lawrence Collections (repr. *Drawings by Old Masters in the British Museum*, vol. III, 1894, pl. 4).   A. C.

Frans Snyders
1579 - 1657

60. *Four Studies of Peacocks*

TECHNIQUE. Pen and brown ink over traces of lead pencil (for the peacocks at either far side), watercolor and gouache (for those at center). (18 x 29.1 cm.). Upper border has been enlarged with a horizontal strip 32 cm. wide.

PROVENANCE. P. J. Mariette; stamp at lower left (Lugt 1852); sale, Paris, 1775, part of lot no. 1038. Bought at this sale for the Royal Collection. Inventory 20.451.

BIBLIOGRAPHY. Lugt, *Flamands*, 1949, vol. II, no. 1303.
Le Cabinet d'un grand amateur, *P. J. Mariette*, Exhibition Catalogue, Paris, Louvre, 1967, no. 204.

Mariette, whose collection included five drawings by Snyders, admired in this "excellent peintre de fruicts et d'animaux... sa touche... légère et spirituelle, ses animaux, surtout les chiens, dessinés avec élégance; il a sçu leur donner un air de vie qu'on ne trouve point ailleurs" (*Abecedario*, V, pp. 240-241).
Snyders is best known for grandiose paintings composed of dead game, live animals, vegetables and fruit, dynamic and at times even moving. The simple subject and unusually denuded composition of the Louvre drawing are therefore somewhat surprising; possibly this was a study from life which preceded a large decorative work.   A. C.

Jacques Fouquières
1590 - 1659

61. *Stream Winding through a Forest Interior*

TECHNIQUE. Brush, watercolor and gouache. (38.1 x 37.7 cm.).

PROVENANCE. P. J. Mariette; stamp at lower right (Lugt 1852); sale, Paris, 1775, no. 1238. Bought at this sale for the Royal Collection. Inventory 19.970.

BIBLIOGRAPHY. W. Stechow, "Drawings and Etchings of J. Fouquières," in *Gazette des Beaux-Arts*, 1948, vol. II, pl. IX.
Lugt, *Flamands*, 1949, vol. I, no. 662, pl. LXV.
Le Cabinet d'un grand amateur, P. J. Mariette, Exhibition Catalogue, Paris, Louvre, 1967, no. 176.

When we consider the expressive and superbly free treatment of this drawing, we can only agree with Mariette for whom Jacques Fouquières was one of the finest landscape artists of his time: "...ce qui me charme dans ce maître, c'est qu'il est expressif et qu'il entre merveilleusement dans le détail des formes; il n'oublie rien. Il y a dans la plupart de ses dessins, des effets de lumière étonnants" (*Abecedario*, II, p. 258).

Fouquières served his apprenticeship in Antwerp with Josse de Momper or Breughel, called "Velvet," and also worked with Rubens before establishing himself in France. In fact, traces of the great Flemish painter are so evident (see no. 54) in this masterly work that one is inclined to assume it was executed during the period of collaboration between the two artists. On the other hand, the breadth of style and skillful balance of the composition might indicate that it dates from a later period, in France, where Fouquières' art, under the influence of the Carracci and Bril, reached its full development. In a painting recently purchased by the Louvre, Fouquières again treats, but in greater detail, the motif of a stream winding through a forest, with touches of light playing on the water (Inventory RF 1950-32).   A. C.

Jacob Jordaens
1593 - 1678

62. *Holy Family by Candlelight*

TECHNIQUE. Black and red chalk, brown wash and watercolor, heightened with white gouache. (44.1 x 41.2 cm.).

PROVENANCE. Dr. Suchet. Mme Juiff; given to the Louvre in 1929. Inventory RF 12.209.

BIBLIOGRAPHY. Lugt, *Flamands*, 1949, vol. I, no. 721, pl. LXXIV.
Dr Ir. R. A. d'Hulst, *De Tekeningen van Jakob Jordaens...*, Brussels, 1956, p. 331, no. 31.
Les plus beaux Dessins du Louvre, Exhibition Catalogue, Paris, Louvre, 1962, no. 48.
Teekeningen van Jakob Jordaens 1593-1678, Exhibition Catalogue, Antwerp-Rotterdam, 1966-1967, no. 25.

This monumental drawing, datable about 1618-1620, belongs to a period when the artist was especially attracted by the effects of light and the realism characteristic of Caravaggio. Though not directly related to a painting, stylistically it resembles certain canvases representing the same subject, notably the *Holy Family with Saint Anne*, which is now in the Detroit Museum (repr. D'Hulst, fig. 18). Here, however, light plays a greater role; contrasting with the shadows, it is used to emphasize volumes and create a more naturally intimate atmosphere. Jordaens frequently used candlelight in his drawings or paintings (*Ecce Homo*, Louvre, Cabinet des Dessins, Inventory 20.023; *Holy Family with Saint Anne*, private collection, New York; *Holy Family*, National Museum, Stockholm; *Holy Family with Shepherds*, private collection, New York, repr. D'Hulst, figs. 63, 49, 9), thereby giving a personal interpretation to the Tenebrist style developed in the XVII century by an international group of artists.

Free from pretense, this homely scene, constructed in terms of masses, is particularly representative of Jordaens' early style. F. Lugt has pointed out an equally forceful drawing in the Albertina.   A. C.

Jacob Jordaens

1593 - 1678

63. *Rest on the Flight into Egypt*

TECHNIQUE. Pen and ink, watercolor, heightened with white, over traces of black chalk. (25.4 x 20.4 cm.). The right border is enlarged by a narrow vertical strip.

PROVENANCE. Acquired by the Louvre during the Revolution. Inventory 20.015.

BIBLIOGRAPHY. M. Rooses, *Jordaens, sa vie et ses œuvres*, Paris, (1906), pp. 27-28, 265.
Lugt, *Flamands*, 1949, vol. I, no. 723, pl. LXXVI.
Dr. Ir. R. A. d'Hulst, *De Tekeningen van Jakob Jordaens...*, Brussels, 1956, p. 281 and no. 161, p. 386.

Though solidly structured, this delicately tinted watercolor, generally dated about 1660, contrasts with the robust style and nocturnal atmosphere of the *Holy Family by Candlelight* (see no. 62), revealing another aspect of Jordaens' art as a draughtsman—his predilection for color.

Rest on the Flight into Egypt may be related or compared to various other known works by Jordaens. The composition of a painting from the Scribe Collection, now in the Ghent Museum, is identical (repr. *Album der Tentoonstelling Jacob Jordaens*, Antwerp, 1905). Stylistically the Louvre drawing resembles the "modello" for a tapestry in Bruges representing the *Widow of Jeroboam before the Prophet Abijah* (repr. D'Hulst, fig. 188); the same pen and ink treatment emphasizing certain basic lines characterizes both works which, moreover, contain two similar details: the donkey and the wide-brimmed hat, worn by the Virgin in one, by the widow of Jeroboam in the other, and also present in an early painting by Jordaens: the *Holy Family with Saint Elisabeth and Saint John* (Brussels Museum; repr. D'Hulst, fig. 3).   A.C.

Anton van Dyck

1599 - 1641

64. *The Seizure of Christ*

TECHNIQUE. Brown wash, squared up in black chalk. (24.1 x 20.9 cm.).

PROVENANCE. Acquired by the Louvre during the Revolution.
Inventory 19.909.

BIBLIOGRAPHY. J. Guiffrey, *Antoine Van Dyck, sa vie et son œuvre*, Paris, 1882,
p. 25, repr.
M. Delacre, "Le Dessin dans l'œuvre de Van Dyck," in *Mémoires de l'Académie
Royale de Belgique*, 2nd series, II, 4, Brussels, 1932, p. 78, repr.
Lugt, *Flamands*, 1949, vol. I, no. 586, pl. LII.
W. Stechow, "Anthony Van Dyck's Betrayal of Christ," in *The Minneapolis
Institute of Arts Bulletin*, 1960, no. 49, pp. 8, 13, fig. 8.
H. Vey, *Die Zeichnungen Anton Van Dycks*, Brussels, 1962, vol. I, no. 84; repr.
vol. II, fig. 114.

This violently lighted drawing is related to one of the most striking religious compositions which Van Dyck executed during the
two or three years preceding his departure for Italy in 1621 : *The
Seizure of Christ*, now in the Prado (repr. G. Glück, *Van Dyck.
Des Meisters Gemälde*, Stuttgart-Berlin, 1931, p. 69). Two slightly
different versions of the Prado painting are also known; one in
the collection of Lord Methuem at Corsham Court (repr. Glück,
p. 79) and another in the Minneapolis Institute of Arts (repr.
Stechow, fig. 1).

The general organization of the present study appears to have
been suggested by Martin de Vos' drawing of the same subject
(now in Brussels; repr. Stechow, fig. 2), but the dramatic intensity
reflects Van Dyck's personal concept. In five other drawings
usually connected with this one (Vey, nos. 79-86), it is possible to
follow the progressive heightening of the feeling of anguish expressed here and the artist's efforts to base the construction of the
scene on increasingly marked contrasts. The tormented character
of the present study, also apparent in the Hamburg Museum
drawing (Vey, vol. II, fig. 115), is emphasized here by sharp light
and tense attitudes in what can be considered one of the most representative examples of Van Dyck's early work.   A.C.

Anton van Dyck
1599 - 1641

65. *Portrait of Theodore van Thulden*

TECHNIQUE. Brown wash over traces of black chalk, heightened with white. (25.8 x 18 cm.). Inscribed in pen and ink at lower center: *Boet* or *Doctor* (?).

PROVENANCE. P. J. Mariette; stamp at lower right (Lugt 1852); sale, Paris, 1775, no. 903. Bought at this sale for the Royal Collection. Inventory 19.907.

BIBLIOGRAPHY. J. Guiffrey, *Antoine Van Dyck, sa vie et son œuvre*, Paris, 1882, repr. p. 121.
M. Delacre, "Recherches sur le rôle du dessin dans l'iconographie de Van Dyck," in *Mémoires de l'Académie Royale de Belgique*, 2nd series, II, 4, Brussels, 1932, pp. 22, 24-25, 77-78.
Lugt, *Flamands*, 1949, vol. I, no. 595, pl. LVIII.
Antoon Van Dyck. Tekeningen en olieverfschetsen, Exhibition Catalogue, Antwerp-Rotterdam, 1960, no. 82, pl. LII.
H. Vey, *Die Zeichnungen Anton Van Dycks*, Brussels, 1962, vol. I, no. 256; vol. II, fig. 313.

The subject of this remarkably free and intensely expressive portrait was the uncle of the painter by the same name and a well-known professor of civil law at the University of Louvain. An engraving in reverse was made from the portrait by Pieter de Jode and published by Martin van den Enden in the album which was to constitute the core of Van Dyck's famous *Iconography*—a series of portraits intended by the artist to evoke the most significant political, scientific, and artistic personalities of his time. Most of these works are now divided among various public and private collections. Usually executed in black chalk and wash, they combine complete frankness and natural elegance in a brilliant testimony to the artist's genius as the creator of a new genre—the aristocratic portrait—which was to strongly influence the art of portraiture both in the Netherlands and abroad.

H. Vey contends that the present drawing was probably executed during one of Van Dyck's two trips to Flanders (autumn 1625 or spring 1635). If the inscription at the lower part of the sheet can be deciphered to read *Doctor*, the portrait may well date from the time of the second voyage, as Thulden was made "Juris Doctor" in 1633.   A. C.

Adam Frans van der Meulen

1632 - 1690

66. *The King's Army in front of the Priory of Fives, near Lille* (detail)

TECHNIQUE. Watercolor (for town in the background), and lead pencil. Central section of a drawing executed on sheets which have been pasted together, measuring: 54.7 x 157.5 cm.

PROVENANCE. Sale, Paris, March 30, 1916, part of lot no. 252. Eggimann. Purchased by the Louvre in 1920.
Inventory RF 4918.

BIBLIOGRAPHY. Lugt, *Flamands*, 1949, vol. I, no. 823; pl. XCIII (central part).

The Louvre's extensive collection of drawings by Van der Meulen, more than one hundred pieces coming mainly from the Eggimann Collection, includes landscapes, views of towns and castles, as well as hunting and cavalry scenes. The large drawing whose central section is reproduced here—one of a number of identified compositions—is in many respects stylistically representative of this "peintre des conquêtes de Louis XIV"; the rapid, free calligraphy of the foreground has the spontaneity of on-the-spot studies, while the colored notations of the landscape background reveal the artist as a subtle colorist.

Executed during the 1667 campaign in Flanders, the drawing depicts an episode in the siege of Lille, in August of that year. In the middleground can be seen the buildings of the Priory of Saint Martin of Fives, whose nearby springs provided water for the town of Lille. Here the royal camp had established its headquarters shortly before the fall of the town. The same buildings reappear in three other drawings by Van der Meulen (Inventory 4919, 4920, 4921). The present work was used for a painting which was engraved by Huchtenburg and Baudouins and sent to Versailles by the Louvre in 1927 (Inventory 1480); in the painting, however, the grouping of the figures is considerably modified.   A. C.

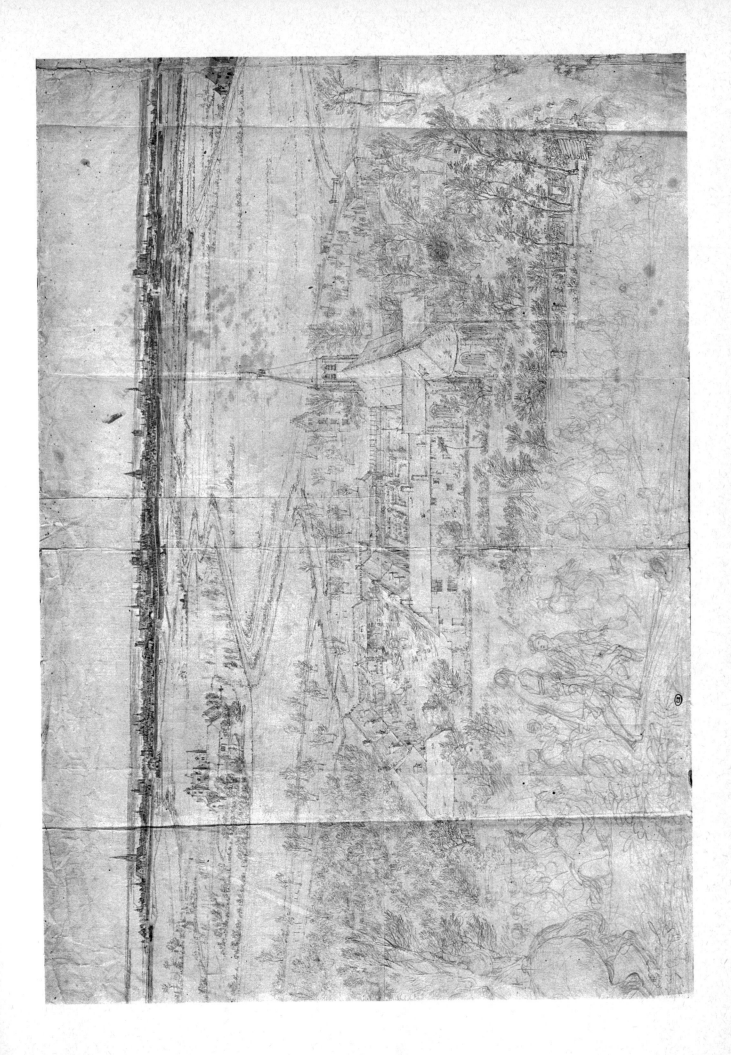

Hieronymus Bosch

About 1450 - 1516

67. *Death of the Miser*

TECHNIQUE. Brush and black ink, heightened with white, on gray prepared paper. (25.6 x 15 cm.). Verso: brush and black ink, study of a helmet and shield; pieces of paper pasted together; inscription in pen and ink at the left: *JERONIMUS BOS VAN ANTWERPEN.*

PROVENANCE. Prince N. Esterhazy; stamp at lower left (Lugt 1965). Count Robiano; sale, Amsterdam, 1926, no. 356. Bought at this sale by A. W. M. Menting; given to the Louvre in 1927.
Inventory RF 6947.

BIBLIOGRAPHY. M. J. Friedländer, *Die altniederländische Malerei*, Berlin, vol. V, 1927, pp. 122-126.
L. von Baldass, *Hieronymus Bosch*, Vienna, 1943, p. 236.
K. G. Boon, "Hieronymus Bosch," in *The Burlington Magazine*, CII, 1960, p. 458.
Ch. de Tolnay, *Hieronymus Bosch*, London, 1966, no. 22, p. 393, repr. p. 328.
Jheronimus Bosch, Exhibition Catalogue, 's-Hertogenbosch, 1967, no. 51, repr.

Both recto and verso of this drawing should be related to the painting by Bosch in the National Gallery in Washington, which is generally thought to be the left panel of a triptych (Tolnay, no. 7, p. 347, repr. p. 91). The theme appears to be the struggle, in the face of death, between Good and Evil, angel and devil, in the manner of scenes from the *Ars Moriendi*. Here, the angel indicates the Cross in an appeal to the dying man, while the devil tempts him with a sack of gold, as Death, with her arrow, is seen opening the door. In the painting, the subject is more clearly defined; the man is represented in the foreground holding a rosary, not shown here, in his left hand; as in the drawing, he reaches with the other hand for the sack of gold which the devil is opening. The composition of the painting is tighter; helmet, shield and lance appear in the foreground rather than at left; the door is placed directly under the window; and the folds of the blanket are treated differently. In spite of these important modifications, the Louvre drawing has been considered a copy, by J. Rosenberg in 1939, and by L. Baldass in 1943, a possibility not excluded by Ch. de Tolnay, though he classified it as an original work in 1966. However, M. J. Friedländer, like A. E. Popham, K. G. Boon and F. Lugt, contends that it is an important and very thoroughly elaborated preparatory drawing intended as the "modello" for a painting. It is usually related to similar drawings, such as the Louvre *Ship of Fools* (Inventory RF 3714; Tolnay, no. 23) and the *Entombment* in the British Museum (A. E. Popham, in the *British Museum Quarterly*, XVII, 1952, p. 45; Tolnay, no. Ia).   R.B.

Hieronymus Bosch

About 1450 - 1516

68. *Studies*

TECHNIQUE. Pen and brown ink. (20.7 x 26.3 cm.). Verso: seven sketches of monsters in the same technique.

PROVENANCE. E. Jabach; paraph on verso (Lugt 2959). Purchased for the Royal Collection in 1671.
Inventory 20.871.

BIBLIOGRAPHY. M. J. Friedländer, *Die altniederländische Malerei*, Berlin, vol. V, 1927, p. 126, pl. LXXVIII.
J. Combe, *Jérôme Bosch*, Paris, 1946, no. 128.
L. Baldass, *Jheronimus Bosch*, Vienna, 1959, pp. 61, 65.
Ch. de Tolnay, *Hieronymus Bosch*, London, 1966, no. 11, p. 390, repr. p. 319.
Jheronimus Bosch, Exhibition Catalogue, 's-Hertogenbosch, 1967, no. 58, repr.

This remarkable sheet, which entered the Royal Collection in the XVII century, is unanimously accepted as an original work by Bosch; the various sketches in the same technique form several groups which may have been executed at different periods. At the lower part of the sheet, turned sideways, the artist evokes a man kneeling beside the pillar of a Gothic church whose arcatures are lightly indicated. The different poses of a seated saint holding a book are studied in four sketches; although no one element permits conclusive identification, Ch. de Tolnay proposed an interesting comparison between this figure and that of Saint Anthony in a painting in the Walter P. Chrysler Collection in New York (Tolnay, no. 21a, repr. p. 254). Tolnay considers both the painting and another drawn representation of the saint, in Berlin, as works attributable to Bosch, though L. Baldass contends that the Berlin drawing is an imitation (*idem*, no. 5, repr. p. 318). Bosch often depicted the theme of the *Temptation of Saint Anthony* which is particularly well suited to the evocation of a demonic world, notably in the famous Lisbon Triptych (*idem*, no. 18, repr. pp. 134–163) and the Prado painting (*idem*, no. 32, repr. p. 306).

In the present sheet, on the recto, around the studies of the saint, and on the verso, strange creatures are seen, gnomes and fantastic monsters endowed with intense vitality by the visionary imagination of their creator. The motif of a glutton devoured by a sea monster, at the upper left of the sheet, reappears in the right wing-panel of the *Last Judgment* in Bruges (*idem*, repr. p. 201).

R. B.

Lucas van Leyden

1494 - 1533

69. *Portrait of a Man Wearing a Wide Brimmed Hat*

TECHNIQUE. Black chalk on cream paper. (26.5 x 32.5 cm.). Sheet cut out at right, top and left, pasted on another sheet of the same color.

PROVENANCE. Probably Paignon-Dijonval; Catalogue, Paris, 1810, no. 1801. N. Révil; sale, Paris, 1842, no. 148. His de la Salle; stamp at lower left (Lugt 1333); given to the Louvre in 1878. Inventory RF 739.

BIBLIOGRAPHY. F. Dülberg, *Lucas van Leyden*, Haarlem (1905), no. 68, repr. N. Beets, *Lucas de Leyde*, Paris-Brussels, 1913, p. 77. *Middeleeuwse Kunst der Noordelijke Nederlanden*, Exhibition Catalogue, Amsterdam, 1958, no. 204. M. J. Friedländer, *Lucas van Leyden*, Berlin, 1963, p. 76, no. 18. *Le Seizième Siècle européen. Dessins du Louvre*, Exhibition Catalogue, Paris, Louvre, 1965, no. 71, pl. XIX.

The portraits of Lucas van Leyden stand out among his drawings for their exceptionally high quality; entirely executed in black chalk, they testify to the acuity of the artist's observations, his authority as a draughtsman and his intelligent understanding of the resources of a technique which he was the first to employ in the Netherlands. In this masterful, highly polished study, precise sensitive indications model the face while the hair and garment are treated more freely. Lucas had already proven himself as a portraitist before Dürer's arrival in the Netherlands in 1520; however, it seems that only after meeting the German master in Antwerp in 1521 did he attempt to vie with him in a series of large studies, of which the present one is undoubtedly the most representative. It is interesting to compare these portraits with those Dürer executed during the same period (see nos. 10, 11). Three other portraits by Lucas, generally dated 1521, are in the Louvre: *Portrait of a Man* (Inventory 19.181; Friedländer, no. 19) and *Portrait of an Old Woman* (Inventory 22.677; Friedländer, no. 21) with the study of a young woman on the verso, reproduced on the next page (no. 70).   R. B.

Lucas van Leyden

1494 - 1533

70. *Portrait of a Young Woman Wearing a Headdress*

TECHNIQUE. Black chalk. (32.1 x 36 cm.). The original sheet has been made rectangular by strips of white paper added at right and left. Recto: portrait of an old woman, in the same technique; inscribed in pen and ink at lower left the initial: *L*; and at the right, the number: *11*.

PROVENANCE. Acquired by the Louvre during the Revolution. Inventory 22.677 verso.

BIBLIOGRAPHY. F. Dülberg, *Lucas van Leyden*, Haarlem (1905), no. 69, repr. (verso).
F. Dülberg, *Frühholländer*, Haarlem (1908), pls. 14-15 (recto and verso).
N. Beets, *Lucas de Leyde*, Paris-Brussels, 1913, p. 77.
M. J. Friedländer, *Lucas van Leyden*, Berlin, 1963, p. 76, no. 21.
Le Seizième Siècle européen. Dessins du Louvre, Exhibition Catalogue, Paris, Louvre, 1965, no. 73, pl. XIX (recto).

Less elaborate than the *Portrait of a Man* reproduced (see no. 69), this study of a young woman has preserved all the spontaneity and freshness of the artist's first impetus. If the sketch of the pleated headdress is barely perceptible, the face is definitely established by shadows indicated with tight, interpenetrating slashes in black chalk which shade off in the lighter parts. The subject's gaze and the firm modeling of her lips are particularly beautiful and confer an extraordinary presence on this calm serious face; the girl's youthfulness seems the more triumphant in contrast with the *Portrait of an Old Woman*, studied on the recto of the same sheet. On the strength of a comparison with the *Portrait of a Woman* in the Staatliche Museum in Weimar, signed and dated 1521 (Friedländer, no. 22), the two Louvre sheets are generally placed during the same period and included among the series of portraits executed by Lucas after he had met Dürer in Antwerp.   R. B.

Hans Bol
1534 - 1593

71. *Saint John the Baptist Preaching*

TECHNIQUE. Gouache, heightened with gold, on vellum stuck on wood. (23.6 x 33 cm.). Signed and dated in gilded letters, at the left on the tree trunk: *Hans Bol 1589*.

PROVENANCE. Entered the Louvre before 1827. Inventory 19.592.

BIBLIOGRAPHY. F. Reiset, *Dessins du Louvre. Ecole allemande, flamande et hollandaise*, Paris, 1866, no. 478.
Le Seizième Siècle européen. Dessins du Louvre, Exhibition Catalogue, Paris, Louvre, 1965, no. 169, pl. XLI.

Groups of standing figures in the foreground, seen from the back, frame the main scene; seated in the shade of several tall trees at the left, Saint John the Baptist is seen preaching to the crowd surrounding him. The simplicity of the saint's pose, the rustic atmosphere and precise rendering of contemporary dress emphasize Bol's homeliness. He is less interested in the sacred nature of the theme than in an abundance of familiar and picturesque details: spectators hanging from the trees, children playing, the dog near the stream and stags bounding through the forest interior—all of which his brush renders effectively. His feeling for nature is expressed in the beautiful landscape at the center, in which a river winds through a valley.

The spirit and harmonious coloration of this work, dated 1589, are characteristic of the series of small format gouaches which had made Bol's fame since 1567. Driven by war from his native town of Maline to Antwerp, Berg-op-Zoom, Dordrecht and Delft, the artist had settled at that time in Amsterdam, where he exerted a definite influence, before dying there in 1593. Bol engraved the same subject, *Saint John the Baptist Preaching*, with a slightly different composition, in a series of twelve circular works (repr. F. W. H. Hollstein, *Dutch and Flemish Etchings, Engravings and Woodcuts, 1450-1700*, Amsterdam, 1949, vol. III, no. 9).   R.B.

Jacob de Gheyn

1565 - 1629

72. *Plucked Chickens Hanging from Nails*

TECHNIQUE. Pen and brown ink. (16.7 x 13.5 cm.).

PROVENANCE. Acquired by the Louvre during the Revolution.

BIBLIOGRAPHY: Lugt, *Hollandais*, vol. I, 1929, no. 284, pl. L.
Intimistes hollandais, Exhibition Catalogue, Paris, Louvre, 1953, no. 23.
Le Bestiaire hollandais, Exhibition Catalogue, Paris, Institut Néerlandais, 1960, no. 88.

Famous during his lifetime for his paintings, Jacob de Gheyn is today known mainly for his graphic and engraved works; thanks to his pen and ink drawings, he is considered one of the most original Dutch artists of the late XVI and early XVII centuries. After serving an initial apprenticeship with his father, a stained glass artist, De Gheyn became the student of Goltzius under whose influence he developed a supple and technically brilliant use of line (see no. 73). In his studies, a tight interplay of pen and ink cross-hatching carefully models forms, revealing his skill as a burin engraver; at the same time, a highly original imagination and evident sensitivity make the least of his sketches an unusually powerful graphic expression.

De Gheyn's studies of animals, birds and insects, combining original, often surprising page-settings with careful observation and treatment, must be considered apart from the rest of his work. A remarkable example of this is the present drawing, whose attribution was established by F. Lugt. Also to be mentioned among this particular group are the *Sea-urchin* in the Rijksmuseum in Amsterdam, the *Storks* in the F. Lugt Collection, as well as studies, heightened with watercolor, of a *Mouse* and a *Crab*, which are part of a series of twenty-two plates executed between 1600 and 1604 for Emperor Rudolph II's Library of Natural History in Prague (Institut Néerlandais, Exhibition Catalogue, 1960, no. 81).   R.B.

Hendrik Goltzius

1558 - 1617

73. *Project for a Fountain*

TECHNIQUE. Pen and brown ink, heightened with watercolor and white. (32.7 x 19.5 cm.). Signed and dated in pen and brown ink on the plinth: *A⁰ H.G. 98.*

PROVENANCE. Acquired by the Louvre during the Revolution. Inventory 22.598.

BIBLIOGRAPHY. Lugt, *Hollandais*, vol. I, 1929, no. 293, pl. LII.
E. K. J. Reznicek, *Die Zeichnungen von Hendrick Goltzius*, Utrecht, 1961, pp. 114-115, no. 158, pp. 300-301, pl. 316.
Hendrick Goltzius als Tekenaar, Exhibition Catalogue, Rotterdam-Haarlem, 1958, no. 123.
Le Seizième Siècle européen. Dessins du Louvre, Exhibition Catalogue, Paris, Louvre, 1965, no. 181, pl. LXVI.

A full-figured woman is seen standing on a turtle flanked by two dolphins; personifying Abundance, she carries a horn filled with flowers and fruit, and with her left hand presses her breast from which water spouts, as it does from the diadem adorning her hair. The sketch at left repeats this motif in right profile, emphasizing the figure's elongated forms and the pronounced sway of the hips. The lively graphic style and exquisitely delicate coloring of this sheet, dated 1598, testify to the refined art of Hendrik Goltzius, founder of the Haarlem Academy and foremost exponent of the Mannerist style in the Netherlands. Imaginative fantasy and decorative skill are the traits shared by the various manifestations of the Mannerist movement in Italy and in Central and Northern Europe; designs for fountains, in particular, became a convenient pretext for extremely whimsical inventions, the project of the Florentine Jacopo Zucchi illustrating the *Birth of Coral*, for example (Louvre, Inventory 4553; repr. Exhibition Catalogue, Louvre, 1965, no. 254, pl. LXIX) or that of the Flemish painter Sustris on the similar theme of *Perseus* (W. Wegner, *Hundert Meister Zeichnungen aus den Staatlichen graphischen Sammlungen*, Munich, 1958, pl. 69)   R.B.

Roelant Savery
1576 - 1639

74. *Landscape with a Man Sketching*

TECHNIQUE. Pen and brown ink. (51.3 x 48.3 cm).

PROVENANCE. E. Jabach; paraph at lower left (Lugt 2961). Purchased for the Royal Collection in 1671.
Inventory 20.721.

BIBLIOGRAPHY. Handwritten manuscript of the Jabach Collection. German and Flemish Schools no. 254.
Lugt, *Hollandais*, vol. II, 1931, no. 710, pl. XL.
Roelandt Savery, Exhibition Catalogue, Ghent, 1954, no. 135, repr.

Born in Courtrai, Savery had established himself in Amsterdam by 1591. In 1604, in Prague, he entered the service of the Emperor Rudolph II, who had already drawn to his court the Flemish painters G. Hoefnagel (see no. 45) and Spranger (see no. 46). In order to further the emperor's project for decorating his palace with landscapes depicting his country's most picturesque sites, Savery was sent to the Tyrol. Inspired by the exceptional beauty of the region, the Northern artist executed a remarkable series of drawings directly from nature. After the death of Rudolph II in 1612, he became a court painter in Vienna, in the service of Rudolph's brother, Emperor Mathias; in 1618, he returned to Utrecht where he died in poverty.

Though Flemish by birth, Savery is related to the Dutch school by the strong influence of his landscape and animal representations among the painters of Holland; Rembrandt, for example, is known to have owned an album of his drawings. Grandiose in its panoramic vision and at the same time extremely precise in detail, this large landscape is a superb example of the style of Savery's pen and ink drawings. A man sits sketching on a rocky slope with his sword unsheathed beside him; an immense plain stretches below, lined with rivers and roads, dotted with houses and clumps of trees—a conception which brings to mind the landscapes of Brueghel (see no. 42). The drawing was engraved by Jac. Matham, with the inscription: *R. Savari effigiavit ad vivum in Bohemia* (Bartsch, 201); in the XVII century, it was classified in the Jabach Collection under the name of Savery, where it was described as "Un grand paysage de rochers où il y a un homme qui desseigne..." In 1671 the drawing entered the Royal Collection, where the attribution was lost and the work incorrectly classified with the Venetian school. F. Lugt restored it to the artist in 1931. R. B.

Jan Harmensz Muller

1571 - 1628

75. *The Masked Ball*

TECHNIQUE. Pen and brown ink, brown wash, heightened with white, on cream paper. (32.6 x 47.6 cm.). Inscribed in pen and ink at lower left: *Jean Muller*.

PROVENANCE. Van Schorel; sale, Amsterdam, 1774, no. 162, pl. 80. Acquired by the Louvre before 1827.
Inventory 20.900.

BIBLIOGRAPHY. Lugt, *Hollandais*, vol. I, 1929, no. 492, pl. LXXXIV.
E. J. K. Reznicek, "Jan Harmensz Muller als Tekenaar," in *Nederlands Kunst-historisch Jaarboek*, 7, 1956, pp. 94-95, no. 33, p. 117, fig. 16.
Concerts et Musiciens, Exhibition Catalogue, Besançon, 1957, no. 109.
Le Seizième Siècle européen. Dessins du Louvre, Exhibition Catalogue, Paris, Louvre, 1965, no. 188, pl. XLVIII.

This drawing is highly characteristic of the Mannerist movement during the early part of the XVII century. Directly influenced by his master Goltzius, Muller was generally connected with the Mannerist circles in Haarlem and Prague and in particular with Spranger whose paintings he engraved. In addition to these determinant influences, he experienced the revelation of Italy, with the refinements of Mannerism's ultimate achievements and the effects of light created by such painters as Barrocci. Traces of the latter's style can frequently be detected in Muller's work after his return from Italy towards 1592.

The fantasy and unreal atmosphere of a ball, particularly a masked ball, seem perfectly attuned to the sensibility of the artists of this period; often treated by Joost van Winghe, the subject reappears in the *Masks*, for example, a painting by W. C. Duyster in the Staatliche Museum in Berlin (*Vie en Hollande au XVIIe siècle*, Exhibition Catalogue, Paris, 1967, no. 114, repr. pl. 44), or again in the *Triumph of Folly* by P. J. Quast, now in the Amsterdam Theater Museum (*idem*, no. 153, repr. pl. 44). Muller's drawing shows the masked guests dancing and talking in a long candle-lit gallery hung with tapestries; on the platform an orchestra is playing. In this large and highly finished work, strongly contrasted light and shadow are rendered by an opposition of brown wash and white heightening, extremely pictorial in its effect, while the sophisticated grace and melancholy animation of the figures recall the art of Bellange. There is a study for this composition in the Fodor Museum in Amsterdam (Reznicek, no. 7, p. 112, repr. fig. 171).   R. B.

Jan van Goyen

1596 - 1656

76. The River Bank

TECHNIQUE. Black chalk, heightened with gray wash. (17.2 x 27.2 cm.).
Signed and dated in black chalk at lower left: *V.G. 1653.*

PROVENANCE. His de la Salle; given to the Louvre in 1878.
Inventory RF 841.

BIBLIOGRAPHY. Both de Tauzia, *Dessins de la collection His de la Salle*, Paris, 1881,
no. 184.
Lugt, *Hollandais*, vol. I, 1929, no. 306, pl. LIV.
Intimistes hollandais, Exhibition Catalogue, Paris, Louvre, 1953, no. 25.

Dated 1653, three years before the artist's death, this drawing
may be considered a typical example of his late style. Using black
chalk scarcely heightened by a few touches of gray wash, he
treats one of his customary subjects: a river bank along which can
be seen a fisherman's house with its sloping roof, men and women
busily sorting fish from traps and baskets, and an approaching
boat. The quiet scene is bathed in a silver-gray atmosphere; reflections play on the calm surface of the water, and mist shrouds
the distant landscape where only the steeple of a church can be
descried. Variations on this subject are found in other works by
Van Goyen of the same year: the *Thatched Cottage on the River
Bank*, a painting in the Leipzig Museum in which the same basket
is seen attached to a reel and half submerged (repr. A. Dobrzycke,
Jan van Goyen, Poznan, 1966, pl. 110); and again in a drawing in
Weimar (repr. *idem*, pl. 107). Towards the end of his career Van
Goyen achieved extraordinary freedom in the interpretation and
execution of his subtly suggestive art; a sense of space, planes,
and light is heightened by the expression of an emotion which
lends a grave and melancholy poetry to the smallest of his
sketches. The Louvre claims three further examples of Van
Goyen's drawings dated 1653: two *River Banks* (Lugt, nos. 307,
312, repr. pl. LV) and a *Mill and Church Rising from a Plain* (*idem*,
no. 308, repr. pl. LV).   R. B.

Bartholomeus Breenbergh

1599 - before 1658

77. *View of Tivoli*

TECHNIQUE. Pen and brown ink, brown wash. (38.3 x 51.6 cm.). Inscribed in pen and brown ink at lower left: *Bartolomeo.*

PROVENANCE. P. Crozat; paraph at lower left (Lugt 2951). Acquired by the Louvre during the Revolution.
Inventory 22.545.

BIBLIOGRAPHY. Lugt, *Hollandais*, vol. I, 1929, no. 171, pl. XXV.

Breenbergh, who had been the student of Abraham Bloemaert in Utrecht, was attracted to Italy very early in his career; one of his first paintings, *Ruins*, now in the Louvre (repr. W. Stechow, "Bartheolomeus Breenbergh," in the *Prussian Jahrbuch*, LI, 1930, fig. 1) is dated 1620, which was probably the year of his arrival in Rome. By 1633, the year of his marriage, he had returned to Amsterdam.

There is no doubt that Breenbergh, who was associated with P. Bril and with C. Poelenburg, his collaborator, was one of the most brilliant personalities in the group of Italianizing Northern artists who were to greatly influence the evolution of the landscape during the first half of the XVII century. In a remarkable series of brown wash studies executed in Rome and its surrounding countryside, Breenbergh manifests his interest in picturesque sites and his talent for rendering the variations of light. In the present view of Tivoli, a foreground of foliage is evoked with vibrant touches; beyond, the sun casts a strong light on the walls of the houses on the opposite bank of the Teverone, which is spanned by a small bridge. The superb treatment of the vegetation covering the slopes of the ravine, the energetic accents and transparent shadows testify to Breenbergh's mastery, while justifying comparison with Claude Lorrain. A drawing in the Metropolitan, executed in the same technique and achieving similar effects, appears to represent the same site (repr. J. Bean, *100 European Drawings in the Metropolitan Museum*, New York, n. d., no. 86). In addition, the Louvre claims another *View of Tivoli* seen from the east, with the cathedral tower (Lugt, no. 170, repr. pl. XXV), as well as a study of neighboring ruins. Both works were used for etchings by J. Both and D'Israel (*idem*, no. 173, pl. XXVI).   R. B.

Rembrandt

1606 - 1669

78. Self-Portrait

TECHNIQUE. Pen and brown ink, brown wash and red chalk, heightened with white. (8.1 x 9.2 cm.). Upper corners trimmed. Signed at left center with the monogram: *R.H.L.*, and dated: *1630*.

PROVENANCE. Given by the painter Jan Weissenbruch to Neville D. Goldsmid in The Hague, April 18, 1866 (inscription on verso); sale, Paris, 1876, no. 137. A. Bovet; sale, Paris, 1885, III, no. 1869, repr. L. Bonnat; stamp at lower left (Lugt 1714); given to the Louvre in 1919. Inventory RF 4663.

BIBLIOGRAPHY. C. Hofstede de Groot, *Die Handzeichnungen Rembrandts*, Haarlem, 1906, no. 708.
W. R. Valentiner, *Rembrandt. Des Meisters Handzeichnungen*, Stuttgart-Berlin, (1925), no. 659.
Lugt, *Hollandais*, vol. III, 1933, no. 1149, pl. XXXIII.
K. Bauch, *Die Kunst des jungen Rembrandt*, Heidelberg, 1933, p. 166.
O. Benesch, *The Drawings of Rembrandt*, London, vol. II, 1954, nos. A, 18a, p. 123, fig. 595.

This portrait belongs to the remarkable group of Rembrandt drawings collected by the painter Léon Bonnat, who gave them to the Louvre in 1919. Only the head and shoulders of the artist are shown; his head is covered with a wide-brimmed hat shielding his forehead. Here he is twenty-four and still in Leyden, where he worked before establishing himself in Amsterdam, in 1632. Psychologically penetrating but somewhat meticulous in its execution, the drawing is accepted as an original by various scholars, notably Hofstede de Groot, Valentiner, F. Lugt, and F. Bauch, who believes it to be a preparatory study for the 1630 etching (Hind, *Etchings*, no. 90). In 1954, however, it was classified by O. Benesh as a studio work.   R. B.

79. *The Head of an Old Man Wearing a Turban and a Bird of Paradise*

TECHNIQUE. Pen and brown ink, brown wash, heightened with white. (17.9 x 16.9 cm.). At upper right, the number: *45* (from the Bonnat album).

PROVENANCE. S. Woodburn; sale, London, 1860, no. 1504. W. Russell. L. Bonnat; stamp at lower left (Lugt 1714); given to the Louvre in 1919. Inventory RF 4688.

BIBLIOGRAPHY. C. Hofstede de Groot, *Die Handzeichnungen Rembrandt*, Haarlem, 1906, no. 731.
W. R. Valentiner, *Rembrandt. Des Meisters Handzeichnungen*, Stuttgart-Berlin, (1925), no. 265.
Lugt, *Hollandais*, vol. III, 1933, no. 1184, pl. XLIX.
O. Benesch, *The Drawings of Rembrandt*, London, vol. I, 1954, no. 158, pp. 43-44. pl. 171.
Rembrandt Tekeningen, Exhibition Catalogue, Rotterdam-Amsterdam, 1956, no. 85, pl. 27.

The study of an old man wearing an Oriental headdress has been connected by W. R. Valentiner and F. Lugt with the composition *Susanna and the Elders*, in which he can be seen watching the young woman bathe from a distance. Rembrandt executed two painted versions of this subject: the first, dated 1637, is now in the Mauritshuis in The Hague (A. Bredius, *The Paintings of Rembrandt*, Vienna-London, 1937, no. 505); the second, dated 1647, is in Berlin (*idem*, no. 516). The figure shown here does not appear in the earlier painting and has been considerably modified in the later one. However, the date 1647 seems too late for the style of the present study. F. Lugt dates it sometime between the two paintings, while O. Benesch, who accepts the identification of the subject, believes it was executed about 1637, with similar studies of *Heads of Old Men* related to the *Susanna* composition (nos. 155-157, repr. figs. 168-170). The Louvre further claims *Two Studies of a Bird of Paradise*, also from the Bonnat donation (Lugt, no. 1195; Benesch, no. 456, fig. 513) and contemporaneous with the study reproduced. All three birds were executed after the bird of paradise mentioned in the inventory of the artist's possessions in 1656 (no. 280, a drawer with a bird of paradise and six fans...).   R. B.

Rembrandt
1606 - 1669

80. *Solomon Worshipping the Idols*

TECHNIQUE. Red chalk. (48.5 x 37.6 cm.). Top of sheet cut to the shape of an arch.

PROVENANCE. Acquired by the Louvre during the Revolution. Inventory 22.970.

BIBLIOGRAPHY. W. R. Valentiner, *Rembrandt. Des Meisters Zeichnungen*, Stuttgart-Berlin, (1925), no. 435.
Lugt, *Hollandais*, vol. III, 1933, no. 1117, pl. VIII.
K. Bauch, *Die Kunst des jungen Rembrandt*, Heidelberg, 1933, p. 227.
O. Benesch, *The Drawings of Rembrandt*, London, I, 1954, no. 136, p. 38, fig. 150.
Rembrandt Tekeningen, Exhibition Catalogue, Rotterdam-Amsterdam, 1956, no. 18, pl. 6.

This large, freely executed red chalk drawing is one of the most authoritative of Rembrandt's early studies inspired from the Old Testament (I, *Kings*, XI). Solomon, wearing a crown, is seen genuflecting before idols inside a gigantic temple; he is surrounded by a rapidly sketched crowd; in the foreground, standing figures, facing the center, frame the scene. Rembrandt lived in daily communion with the world of the Bible. A deeply religious nature enabled him to draw Biblical scenes with a gripping sincerity and sense of life. On the basis of a comparison with a drawing in the same technique dated 1630, in the British Museum, the *Resurrection of Lazarus*, which Rembrandt transformed into an *Entombment of Christ* (Benesch, no. 17, fig. 15), F. Lugt attributes the Louvre drawing to Rembrandt's earliest period, in Leyden. O. Benesch, however, finds it freer of the influence of the artist's masters, notably Lastman and Pynas, and stylistically more developed than the works executed before Rembrandt's departure for Amsterdam in 1632. Comparing it to the red chalk *Ecce Homo* in Dresden (no. 135, repr. fig. 149), he therefore prefers to date it later, about 1637.

Rembrandt
1606 - 1669

81. *Jacob's Dream*

TECHNIQUE. Pen and brown ink, heightened slightly with white. (25 x 20.2 cm.). Inscribed at lower right in a later hand: *R.13*.

PROVENANCE. P. J. Mariette; stamp at lower left (Lugt 1852) and mounted with: *REMBRANDT* inscribed in a cartouche; sale, Paris, 1775, probably part of lot no. 978. Probably acquired by the Louvre during the Revolution. Inventory 22.881.

BIBLIOGRAPHY. C. Hofstede de Groot, *Die Handzeichnungen Rembrandts*, Haarlem, 1906, no. 591.
W. R. Valentiner, *Rembrandt. Des Meisters Handzeichnungen*, Stuttgart-Berlin, (1925), no. 72.
Lugt, *Hollandais*, vol. III, 1933, no. 1111, pl. IV.
O. Benesch, *The Drawings of Rembrandt*, London, vol. III, 1955, no. 557, p. 159, fig. 686.
Le Cabinet d'un grand amateur, P. J. Mariette, Exhibition Catalogue, Paris, Louvre, 1967, no. 192.

Reality and the supernatural blend with an ease achieved only by Rembrandt in the clear balanced composition of this remarkable sheet. Jacob is seen sleeping in a simple attitude at the center, his head resting on his joined hands; his staff propped against the stump of a tree and his flask and bag on the ground constitute a still-life at the right, which has a direct and familiar quality, while an intense spirituality emanates from the angels seen bending over the sleeper with wings outspread. F. Lugt dates the drawing between 1638 and 1642, relating it to the sheet in the Boymans Museum in Rotterdam (Benesch, no. 558, repr. fig. 687) which shows the same scene with a few modifications, in particular, the introduction of a group of cherubs at the center. O. Benesch dates both works later, in 1644, comparing them to the *Good Samaritan* in Berlin, which bears this date and contains zigzag elements similar to those apparent here (*idem*, no. 556, repr. fig. 685). It is interesting to note that in the XVIII century, the Louvre *Jacob's Dream* was admired and etched by the Count de Caylus; it belonged to Mariette whose correct attribution to Rembrandt is inscribed in the cartouche of his blue mount, which has been preserved. Acknowledging nothing superior in the XVII century to the grand style of the Carracci and Poussin, Mariette found in Rembrandt "ni la justesse des proportions ni la noblesse des expressions" (*Abecedario*, IV, p. 349); however, he could not remain indifferent to the exceptional quality of works such as this, or the *View of the Singel Canal* (see no. 87). Eleven drawings by Rembrandt and all his engravings were catalogued in the Mariette sale in 1775.   R. B.

Rembrandt
1606 - 1669

82. *The Good Samaritan at the Door of the Inn*

TECHNIQUE. Pen and brown ink, brown wash. (17.7 x 22.2 cm.). Inscribed at lower left in a later hand: *Le Samaritain paye l'hoste qui le remercie.*

PROVENANCE. Acquired by the Louvre during the Revolution. Inventory 22.883.

BIBLIOGRAPHY. H. de Chennevières, *Dessins du Louvre. Ecoles flammande, hollandaise et allemande*, Paris, (1882), *Rembrandt*, pl. 6.
C. Hofstede de Groot, *Die Handzeichnungen Rembrandts*, Haarlem, 1906, no. 606.
Teekeningen van Oude Meesters der Hollandsche School, Haarlem, Kleinmann, n.d., V, pl. 43.
Lugt, *Hollandais*, vol. III, 1933, no. 1137, pl. XXIV.

The parable of the *Good Samaritan* deeply touched Rembrandt's evangelical soul and particularly engaged his attention between 1640 and 1650; one of his most beautiful drawings inspired from this subject, the *Good Samaritan Tending a Wounded Man*, in the Berlin Kupferstichkabinett, bears the date 1644 (Benesch, no. 556, repr. fig. 685). According to the inscription in French on the drawing reproduced here, probably made in the XVIII century and in a hand which reappears on another Louvre sheet, *Ruth and Booz* (Lugt, no. 1114, repr. pl. VI), the scene seems to represent the Samaritan paying the innkeeper as he leaves. However, as F. Lugt points out, the fact that the scene takes place at night would indicate that the Samaritan is arriving rather than leaving. The right part, freely sketched in brown wash, appears to be unfinished, since the wounded man is not shown strapped to the horse, as in two more thoroughly elaborated drawings representing this incident, in the British Museum and the Boymans Museum (Benesch, nos. 518a and b, repr. figs. 646 and 647). Another sheet, belonging to Captain Weld Blundell, in Hightown (*idem*, no. 629a, fig. 760) shows the Samaritan paying the inkeeper inside the inn. R. B.

amaritain paye l'hoste qui le remercie

Rembrandt
1606 - 1669

83. *Christ upon the Cross between the Two Thieves*

TECHNIQUE. Pen and brown ink, brown wash, heightened with white. (20.8 x 28.5 cm.).

PROVENANCE. Acquired by the Louvre during the Revolution. Inventory 22.885.

BIBLIOGRAPHY. C. Hofstede de Groot, *Die Handzeichnungen Rembrandts*, Haarlem, 1906, no. 609.
W. R. Valentiner, *Rembrandt. Des Meisters Handzeichnungen*, Stuttgart-Berlin, (1925), no. 489.
Lugt, *Hollandais*, vol. III, 1933, no. 1138, pl. XXV.
O. Benesch, *The Drawings of Rembrandt*, London, vol. III, 1955, no. 652, p. 180, fig. 789.

The crosses stand on a hill at the left from which the Temple of Jerusalem is perceptible; the sponge on the end of a spear is being offered to the dying Christ, seen turned to the right in profile. The scene is sketched in a firm rapid style, in pen and ink, barely heightened in certain parts with touches of brown wash. A few unifying indications endow the figures at the foot of the Cross and the group of horsemen at the right with intense vitality. This is a remarkable example of the master's great scenes illustrating the different episodes of the *Passion;* the dramatic tension and epic quality of these scenes reach a climax in the etching of the *Three Crosses* (Hind, *Etchings*, 270).

The present composition is related to the *Calvary* in the Nationalmuseum in Stockholm (Benesch, no. 924, repr. fig. 1137) and to the Berlin *Deposition*, in which a spectator is seen from the back (*idem*, no. 922, repr. fig. 1133), as in this sheet. Another drawing, in the Bibliothèque Nationale in Paris, executed during the same period and stylistically very similar, shows a soldier piercing the heart of Christ upon the Cross (*idem*, no. 653, repr. fig. 790). The drawing reproduced is dated between 1650 and 1655 by F. Lugt and about 1649 by O. Benesch.   R. B.

Rembrandt
1606 - 1669

84. *Zacharias Inscribing the Name of Saint John the Baptist*

TECHNIQUE. Pen and brown ink, brown and gray wash. (19.9 x 31.4 cm.).
Inscribed at lower right, in a later hand: *Rembrandt*.

PROVENANCE. Acquired by the Louvre during the Revolution.
Inventory 22.892.

BIBLIOGRAPHY. C. Hofstede de Groot, *Die Handzeichnungen Rembrandts*,
Haarlem, 1906, no. 601.
W. R. Valentiner, *Rembrandt. Des Meisters Handzeichnungen*, Stuttgart-Berlin,
(1925), no. 272.
Rembrandt, Exhibition Catalogue, Amsterdam, 1932, no. 309.
Lugt, *Hollandais*, vol. III, 1933, no. 1125, pl. XV.
O. Benesch, *The Drawings of Rembrandt*, London, vol. V, 1957, no. 1007, p. 288,
fig. 1219.

Seated beside the bed in which Saint Elisabeth lies holding the child, Zacharias inscribes the name of his son, John the Baptist, on a tablet (*Saint Luke*, I, 63). This work marks the classical tendency of the grand style developed by Rembrandt in his maturity, after 1650. The composition centers on the figure of the old man surrounded by three old women standing; it is balanced at the left by the mass of the curtained bed, which is animated by the interplay of light and shadow, and on the right by the draped table in the background. The contrast between the stability of the clearly defined volumes and the expressive suppleness of the attitudes is apparent in other drawings from the same period, notably the *Holy Women at the Tomb* in the Boymans Museum in Rotterdam (Benesch, no. 1009, repr. fig. 1223). Here, the monumental effects obviously sought by the artist harmonize felicitously with familiar details and the atmosphere of meditative intimacy. F. Lugt dates the drawing between 1650 and 1656, O. Benesch towards 1656; it must be pointed out that in 1654, Rembrandt himself became the father of a daughter, Cornelia.

It is interesting to compare the Louvre drawing of the same subject by one of Rembrandt's students with the master's work (Lugt, no. 1255, repr. pl. LXXVI).   R. B.

Rembrandt
1606 - 1669

85. *Jan Six Writing at IJmond*

TECHNIQUE. Pen and brown ink, brown wash, heightened with white. (13.5 x 19.7 cm.). Upper corners rounded off.

PROVENANCE. Ravaisson-Mollien; sale, Paris, 1903, no. 39. E. Moreau-Nélaton; bequeathed to the Louvre in 1927.
Inventory RF 11.476.

BIBLIOGRAPHY. C. Hofstede de Groot, *Die Handzeichnungen Rembrandts*, Haarlem, 1906, no. 51.
F. Lugt, *Wandelingen met Rembrandt in en om Amsterdam*, 1915, p. 147, pl. 93.
W. R. Valentiner, *Rembrandt. Des Meisters Handzeichnungen*, Stuttgart-Berlin, (1925), no. 738.
Lugt, *Hollandais*, vol. III, 1933, no. 1152, pl. XXXIII.
O. Benesch, *The Drawings of Rembrandt*, London, vol. V, 1957, no. 1172, fig. 1398.

The model, shown writing, is probably Rembrandt's friend and patron, Jan Six. In 1915, F. Lugt was able to identify the landscape seen through the open window; in the foreground is the dike known as the Diemerdijk, bordering the waters of the IJ, which joins the Zuyderzee at this point; the steeple of Schellinwou Church rises on the opposite bank. Here, at IJmond, Jan Six owned a small estate. In this famous drawing, the half-light of the room contrasts with the intense luminosity of the exterior view, freely evoked in pen and ink alone, in the allotted space; a child's face seen against the light, looking through the casement window, establishes the relationship between exterior and interior. The landscape reappears in a contemporary drawing, now in the Boymans Museum in Rotterdam (Benesch, no. 138, repr. fig. 1593), in which the same sailboat is shown anchored on the opposite bank. F. Lugt dates both drawings between 1650 and 1653, when Jan Six and Rembrandt enjoyed a particularly close friendship. O. Benesch further recognizes Jan Six at IJmond in a Munich drawing representing a man wearing a similar hat, seated in a room, reading near a window (*idem*, no. 1173, repr. fig. 1400); in both the Louvre and Munich drawings, the artist's intention is not so much to describe the model's features as to place him in his setting by recreating the atmosphere around him.   R. B.

Rembrandt
1606 - 1669

86. *Portrait of a Man*

TECHNIQUE. Brush and brown ink, reworked in parts by the artist in white gouache. (24.7 x 19.2 cm.). Verso: study of a man in another hand.

PROVENANCE. Inventory 22.919.

BIBLIOGRAPHY. C. Hofstede de Groot, *Die Handzeichnungen Rembrandts*, Haarlem, 1906, no. 632.
W. R. Valentiner, *Rembrandt. Des Meisters Handzeichnungen*, Stuttgart-Berlin, (1925), no. 743.
Lugt, *Hollandais*, vol. III, 1933, no. 1153, pl. XXV.
O. Benesch, *The Drawings of Rembrandt*, London, vol. V, 1957, no. 1182, p. 332, fig. 1408.
Rembrandt Tekeningen, Exhibition Catalogue, Rotterdam-Amsterdam, 1956, no. 253, pl. 70.

This work is unanimously considered one of the most beautiful portraits executed by Rembrandt towards the end of his career. The model, whose features somewhat resemble Jan Six, as F. Lugt points out, is represented almost frontally, wearing dark clothes and a wide-brimmed hat; he stands out against the reserved background of the paper, which bears no indication of a setting. Treated in vigorous strokes of brown wash, freely applied with a brush, the work has the spontaneity of a painter's first sketch, executed rapidly with perfect skill. Unlike most of Rembrandt's drawings, which have suffered from overexposure to light, this sheet has preserved the brilliancy of its colors and the vigor of its contrasts.

The *Portrait of a Young Man* in the Stix-Stichting Collection in Amsterdam must be mentioned in connection with the present portrait since the placement of the figure in the Amsterdam sheet, who may be Rembrandt's son, Titus, is almost identical (Benesch, no. 1181, repr. fig. 1407; Exhibition Catalogue, 1956, no. 253a). F. Lugt dates the two, probably contemporaneous portraits between 1654 and 1658; O. Benesch prefers to situate them later, towards 1662-1665.   R. B.

Rembrandt

1606 - 1669

87. *View of the Singel Canal at Amersfoort*

TECHNIQUE. Pen and brown ink, brown wash. (15.3 x 27.7 cm.). Inscribed in pen and ink at lower left, the initial: *R*; and at the right, the number: *327.*

PROVENANCE. P. J. Mariette; stamp at lower right and at the left (Lugt 1852); sale, Paris, 1775, probably part of lot no. 979. Acquired by the Louvre during the Revolution.
Inventory 22.896.

BIBLIOGRAPHY. F. Lugt, *Mit Rembrandt in Amsterdam*, Berlin, 1920, pp. 157-158, fig. 110.
O. Benesch, *The Drawings of Rembrandt*, London, vol. IV, 1955, no. 824, fig. 971.
Rembrandt Tekeningen, Exhibition Catalogue, Rotterdam-Amsterdam, 1956, no. 120.
J. G. van Gelder, *Prenten en Tekeningen*, Amsterdam, 1958, pl. 65.
Le Cabinet d'un grand amateur, P. J. Mariette, Exhibition Catalogue, Paris, Louvre, 1967, no. 193, repr.

F. Lugt recognized in this famous drawing a view of the Singel Canal at Amersfoort in the Province of Utrecht. By identifying the different sites represented in a series of landscapes and views of towns, F. Lugt reconstituted the itinerary of a trip he believes Rembrandt took between 1650 and 1660, which led the artist as far east as Arnhem; the towns of Muiderberg, Utrecht and Rhenen particularly attracted Rembrandt's attention. O. Benesch finds differences in the works in this series which suggest the possibility of two trips to the same places, the first towards 1647-1648, of which the Louvre drawing would be the most beautiful attestation, the second, a few years later, towards 1652-1653, during which the *View of the Door of the Rhine at Rhenen*, also in the Louvre, could have been executed (Lugt, no. 1198, repr. pl. LVII).

Already in the XVIII century, the masterly execution of this sketch retained the attention of P. J. Mariette, who prized Rembrandt's landscapes above other aspects of the artist's work and acquired this one for his collection. The bold treatment of the trees in the foreground vigorously striped in pen and ink and the delicate touches of brown wash that render the shimmering waters and shadows in the background combine to create an image at once faithful to reality and intensely lyric.   R. B.

Rembrandt
1606 - 1669

88. *Young Man Holding a Flower*

TECHNIQUE. Pen and brown ink, brown wash. (17.5 x 11.8 cm.).

PROVENANCE. G. Huquier; stamp at lower right (Lugt 1285). Acquired by the Louvre during the Revolution.
Inventory 22.917.

BIBLIOGRAPHY. C. Hofstede de Groot, *Die Handzeichnungen Rembrandts*, Haarlem, 1906, no. 634.
W. R. Valentiner, *Rembrandt. Des Meisters Handzeichnungen*, Stuttgart-Berlin, (1925), no. 718.
Lugt, *Hollandais*, vol. III, 1933, no. 1153, repr. pl. XXV.
De Jérôme Bosch à Rembrandt, Exhibition Catalogue, Brussels, 1937, no. 71, pl. XLVII.
O. Benesch, *The Drawings of Rembrandt*, London, vol. V, 1957, no. 1184, p. 333, fig. 1409.

F. Lugt believes that Rembrandt may have portrayed his son, Titus, here, probably between 1658 and 1660. The same denuded style and penetrating acuity reappear in the famous studies for the *Syndics of the Cloth Hall (De Staalmeesters)*, a painting executed in 1662, now in the Rijksmuseum in Amsterdam: the *Seated Staalmeester* in the Rijksprentenkabinet (Benesch, no. 1179, repr. fig. 1401) and the *Standing Staalmeester* in the Boymans Museum (*idem*, no. 1180, repr. fig. 1402). O. Benesch, on the other hand, feels that Rembrandt's art has reached its fullest development in this drawing, possibly his last, which would exclude the possibility of Titus as the model. However, the problem of identifying the figure seems secondary, since this is not so much the portrait of a young man as a poetic and profoundly melancholic evocation of youth itself. A few indications in pen and ink, rubbed with the finger and almost blurred, suggest rather than describe the features of the face and attitude of the figure; the intensity of the gaze and, above all, the hand within a luminous halo extending a flower towards the observer contrast with the evanescent treatment of the young man.   R. B.

Jan Lievens
1607 - 1674

89. *Portrait of a Young Man*

TECHNIQUE. Black chalk and estompe. (19.5 x 21.2 cm.). Inscribed in pen and brown ink at lower right, the number: *9*.

PROVENANCE. Entered the Louvre before 1827.
Inventory 22.394.

BIBLIOGRAPHY. Lugt, *Hollandais*, vol. I, 1929, no. 414, pl. LXXI.
Intimistes Hollandais, Exhibition Catalogue, Paris, Louvre, 1953, no. 31.

Lievens studied under Joris van Schooten in Leyden, his birthplace, and under Pieter Lastman in Amsterdam; Rembrandt, one year his senior, was his friend, and the master's ascendancy is evident in the younger artist's first works. He is to undergo other influences during his stays in England from 1632 to 1634 and in Antwerp between 1635 and 1643, in particular that of Van Dyck. Lievens' graphic work includes interesting landscapes, generally executed in a reed pen and ink; the Louvre claims a beautiful example of these with the *View of a Fenced Wood*, which belonged to Mariette in the XVIII century (Inventory 22.727; Lugt, no. 417, repr. pl. LXX). However, Lievens was above all a great portraitist, as evidenced by his objective yet sensitive black chalk studies. Many of his portraits—those of *Jacob Matham, Daniel Seghers* and *Constantin Huygens* in the British Museum (A. M. Hind, *Drawings by Rembrandt and His School...*, London, 1915, nos. 1, 4, 6, repr. pls. LI and LII), of *Johan Uytenbogaert*, dated 1650, in the Fodor Museum (repr. J. Q. van Regteren Altena, *Dessins de Maîtres Hollandais du XVIIe siècle*, Basel, pl. 26) or *Gaspard Streso*, undoubtedly his masterpiece, in the F. Lugt Collection (repr. J. G. van Gelder, *Prenten en Tekeningen*, Amsterdam, 1958, pl. 89)—equal the works of Cornelis Visscher (see no. 97) in sobriety and sincerity and have something of Van Dyck's distinction (see no. 65); all these qualities are apparent in the likeness of this young stranger.

R. B.

Adriaan van Ostade
1610 - 1685

90. *The Bleeding of the Pig*

TECHNIQUE. Pen and brown ink, gray wash, over a sketch in black chalk. (17.2 x 14.2 cm.). Some contours pricked for transfer.

PROVENANCE. W. Esdaile; purchased by him in 1834; paraphs on recto (Lugt 2617) and verso (Lugt 816 and 2617); sale, London, 1840, no. 845. His de la Salle; stamp at lower right (Lugt 1332); given to the Louvre in 1878. Inventory RF 681.

BIBLIOGRAPHY. Both de Tauzia, *Dessins de la collection His de la Salle*, Paris, 1881, no. 200.
H. de Chennevières, *Dessins du Louvre. Ecoles flamande, hollandaise et allemande*, Paris, n.d., repr. p. 29.
Lugt, *Hollandais*, vol. II, 1931, no. 506, pl. VI.

This drawing is a preparatory study for a watercolor in the Fodor Museum in Amsterdam (repr. *Handzeichnungen alter Meister Hollaendischen Schule*, Kleinmann, III, pl. 19). Van Ostade's richly colored and highly polished genre scenes in watercolor, conceived in the manner of a small format painting, were extremely popular among art lovers of his period; however, his qualities as a draughtsman are affirmed more directly in his rapidly executed studies. Here, over the brief black chalk sketch, an agitated pen indicates the grouping of figures: the three busy men, the circle of children and a woman coming forth against the light from the open door at the left. Touches of gray wash distribute light and shadow in this domestic scene. The ladder standing against the wall and the handsome still life of the barrel and basket in the foreground at the right emphasize Van Ostade's keen observation of everyday life and his feeling for precise, veracious details which make his portrayal of country and village life highly convincing. The same subject, slightly modified, appears in a drawing in the Royal Museum in Brussels (repr. *120 Dessins flamands et hollandais*, Exhibition Catalogue, Brussels, 1967, no. 99).   R. B.

Gerard Dou

1613 - 1675

91. *Portrait of the Artist's Mother*

TECHNIQUE. Black and red chalk, heightened with white; oval border in black chalk and brown wash. (19.1 x 16.8 cm.). Signed and dated in black chalk at left: *G. Dou 1638.*

PROVENANCE. J. Tonneman; sale, Amsterdam, 1754, Album N, no. 26. S. Feitama; sale, Amsterdam, 1758. W. Baillie. J. D. Nijman. H. van Eyl Sluyter; sale, Amsterdam, 1814, Album G, no. 11. N. Revil; sale, Paris, 1845, no. 21. Bought at this sale by the Louvre.
Inventory 22.579.

BIBLIOGRAPHY. W. Martin, *Het Leven en de Werken van Gerrit Dou*, Leyden, 1901, p. 245, no. 371.
Lugt, *Hollandais*, vol. I, 1929, no. 248, pl. XXXIX.
M. D. Henckel, *Le Dessin Hollandais*, Paris, 1931, p. 90.
De Jérôme Bosch à Rembrandt, Exhibition Catalogue, Brussels, 1937, no. 97, pl. LXI.
W. Bernt, *Die Niederländischen Zeichner des 17. Jahrhunderts*, Munich, 1957, no. 91, repr.

Gerard Dou executed this handsome portrait of his mother in 1638. The same model reappears in a similar pose in the *Self Portrait*, in the Brunswick Museum, in which the artist is seen holding a small portrait or perhaps a mirror representing three members of his family (repr. W. Martin, *Gerard Dou. Des Meisters Gemälde*, Stuttgart-Berlin, 1913, pl. 18). His mother is portrayed alone, at different ages, in several paintings, the most remarkable of which is in the Cook Collection in Richmond (*idem*, pl. 45). Originally from Leyden, like Rembrandt, Dou was the master's first student; his genre scenes, carefully executed with refined chromatic effects, brought him fame within his lifetime and a place among the foremost Leyden artists. The fact that few of the artist's drawings are presently known makes this study all the more interesting; sensitive red chalk notations are blended with black chalk shadows, a technique which Dou used again, notably in the *Old Woman with a Muff* in the British Museum (repr. Henckel, pl. LXXXV) and in the *Man Cutting a Quill* in the Fodor Museum in Amsterdam (repr. J. H. S. Mellaart, *Dutch Drawings of the Seventeenth Century*, London, 1926, pl. 57). The importance of the Louvre drawing was soon recognized. F. Lugt traced its history from the Tonneman sale in Amsterdam in 1754 to its purchase by the Louvre in 1845. In 1775, one of the work's successive owners, W. Baillie in London, engraved it in facsimile (*The Works of Captain William Baillie after Paintings and Drawings by the Greatest Masters*, pl. 10). R. B.

Ferdinand Bol
1616 - 1680

92. *Family Portrait*

TECHNIQUE. Pen and brown ink, brown and gray wash. (18.7 x 26.4 cm.).
Signed and dated in pen and ink at upper left: *J. Bol f. 1642.*

PROVENANCE. A. L. Tolling; sale, Amsterdam, 1768, Album B, no. 103. Nijman; sale, Paris, 1776, no. 104. J. Gildemeester; sale, Amsterdam, 1800, no. 42.
A. Mouriau; stamps on verso (Lugt 1829) and recto (Lugt 1853); sale, Paris, 1858, no. 38. His de la Salle; stamp at lower right (Lugt 1333); given to the Louvre in 1878.
Inventory RF 647.

BIBLIOGRAPHY. Both de Tauzia, *Dessins de la collection His de la Salle*, Paris, 1881, no. 157.
Lugt, *Hollandais*, vol. I, 1929, no. 123, pl. XVIII.
Intimistes hollandais, Exhibition Catalogue, Paris, Louvre, 1957, no. 61.

Ferdinand Bol's drawings of Biblical or historical subjects reflect, at times too faithfully, his admiration for Rembrandt, with whom he studied and worked for several years after 1631. This is not true of the Louvre *Family Portrait*, executed in 1642; one of the artist's rare signed and dated works, it provides a good example of his personal style in the field of his greatest success. In fact, during his lifetime, Bol's reputation as a portraitist surpassed Rembrandt's, and some of his creations, like the *Portrait of Elisabeth Bas*, a painting in the Rijksmuseum in Amsterdam, display unquestionable merit.

Here, Bol has placed the members of a family in the framework of their daily existence, a book-lined study with a window opening onto houses below a steeple; the father sits behind a table covered by a rug, with his son near him; the mother, at the right, is surrounded by her three daughters. The atmosphere of the scene is faithfully evoked and the furnishings and clothes precisely detailed, in this exceptionally interesting record of everyday life in Holland during the second quarter of the XVII century.   R. B.

Gerbrand van den Eeckhout
1621 - 1674

93. *View of a Canal*

TECHNIQUE. Watercolor over a sketch in black chalk. (14 x 18.6 cm.). Signed in pen and ink at the left, on the barge's rudder: *G. V. Eeckhout.*

PROVENANCE. Probably C. Elout; sale, Haarlem, 1780, Album B, no. 99. Probably H. van Maarseveen; sale, Amsterdam, 1793, Album H, no. 31. Ploos van Amstel; stamp on verso (Lugt 2034); sale, Amsterdam, 1800, Album E, no. 5. J. C. Pruyssenaar; sale, Amsterdam, 1804, Album B, no. 30. Van Eyl Sluyter; sale, Amsterdam, 1814, Album A, no. 31. Molkenboer; sale, Amsterdam, 1825, Album A, no. 16. G. van Franckenstein; sale, Amsterdam, 1833, Album A, no. 31. I. van Idsinga; sale, Amsterdam, 1840, Album E, no. 2. His de la Salle; stamp at lower left (Lugt 1333); given to the Louvre in 1878.

BIBLIOGRAPHY. Lugt, *Hollandais*, vol. I, 1929, no. 261, pl. XLIII. *Intimistes hollandais*, Exhibition Catalogue, Paris, Louvre, 1953, no. 18.

Gerbrand van den Eeckhout, undoubtedly one of Rembrandt's most talented students, worked with the master between 1635 and 1640. Though his religious scenes show the direct influence of his teacher, his studies of figures and landscapes bear the mark of his own personality. His expressive and synthetical treatment of the *Woman Spinning* in the Rijksmuseum (repr. W. Bernt, *Die Nieder-ländischen Zeichner des 17. Jahrhunderts*, Munich, 1957, no. 208) and the famous *Young Boy Leaning on a Chair* in the Albertina lends these works an exceptionally poetic intensity; his landscapes, in brown wash, such as the *View of the Château de Clèves*, dated 1650, in Berlin (repr. *idem*, no. 210), or those in watercolor, such as the *View of Gorkum*, about 1660, in the F. Lugt Collection (repr. *Old Master Drawings*, March 1929, pl. LXI) demonstrate the intelligence of his composition and the diversity of his means of expression.

The Louvre drawing represents part of the canal lined with pink brick houses and shaded by trees, perhaps at Delft, whose town hall steeple is recognizable at the right; two men hoop a barrel on a moored barge, the stern of which is covered with canvas sheets, while a black cat watches birds from a window sill. The simplicity and luminosity of this little scene reveal a pre-Impressionist sensibility.   R. B.

Lambert Doomer

1622 - 1700

94. *A View near Amboise*

TECHNIQUE. Brown wash with watercolor heightening over a sketch in black chalk, traces of pen and brown ink. (19.5 x 30.3 cm.). Signed in pen and ink at lower left: *Doomer f.* Inscribed in pen and ink on verso: *bij Amboose Aen de Loore* (near Amboise on the Loire).

PROVENANCE. Entered the Louvre before 1827.
Inventory 23.002.

BIBLIOGRAPHY. Lugt, *Hollandais*, vol. I, 1929, pl. XXXVI.
H. M. van den Berg, "Willem Schellinx en Lambert Doomer in Frankrijk," in *Oudheidkundig Jaarboek*, XI, 1942, p. 25, no. 4, pl. 24.
Rembrandt als Leermeester, Exhibition Catalogue, Leyden, 1956, no. 97.

This is a remarkable example of the art of this great landscapist, who studied under Rembrandt after 1640. Doomer travelled a great deal in Germany, Switzerland, Italy and England. His itineraries can be reconstructed thanks to his sketchbook, which he used as a travel diary. In 1645, he went to France to visit his two brothers living in Nantes; the town and surrounding countryside inspired him to draw a series of beautiful landscapes, now in Oxford (K. T. Parker, *Drawings in the Ashmolean Museum*, Oxford, vol. I, 1938, no. 127, repr. pl. XXV) and Berlin (E. Bock and J. Rosenberg, *Die Niederländischen Meister*, Berlin, 1930, vol. I, nos. 1175, 1194, 2616). Accompanied by Willem Schellinks (see no. 95), he stayed on the banks of the Loire, lingering in Saumur, Amboise and Angers, where he painted the Pont Neuf in a work now in the Louvre. Doomer's drawings reveal his interest in the picturesque sites he came upon during his travels and in the old monuments he depicted with a precision that never becomes dry; it is always tempered by a romantic sensibility which lends his works a unique quality. Here, the strange dwellings in the rocks near Amboise have retained the artist's attention; authoritative indications in black chalk construct the different planes; contrasts are emphasized with energetic brown touches of watercolor in the range of sober colors peculiar to Doomer. A drawing of the same subject is in the Kupferstichkabinett in Berlin (Bock and Rosenberg, no. 369).   R. B.

Willem Schellinks

About 1627 - 1678

95. *View of the Port of Valletta in Malta*

TECHNIQUE. Pen and brown ink, brown and green wash, over traces of black chalk. (40.1 x 58 cm.). Signed and dated in pen and brown ink at lower right: *W. Schillinks Ft. ad vivum Malta 1664.*

PROVENANCE. J. Tonneman; sale, Amsterdam, 1754, Album B, no. 12. Huquier; sale, Paris, 1772, no. 253. P. J. Mariette; sale, Paris, 1775, no. 1035. Bought at this sale for the Royal Collection.
Inventory 23.024.

BIBLIOGRAPHY. Lugt, *Hollandais*, vol. II, 1931, no. 718, pl. XLII.
W. Bernt, *Die Niederländischen Zeichner des 17. Jahrhunderts*, Munich, 1958, vol. II, no. 539, repr.
Le Cabinet d'un grand amateur, P. J. Mariette, Exhibition Catalogue, Paris, Louvre, 1967, no. 203.

A student of Karel Dujardin, Schellinks was a painter, draughtsman, engraver and also a poet. Like several XVII century Dutch artists, he was a zealous traveller, to England, Germany, France, which he visited with Lambert Doomer (see no. 94), and Italy. He returned from these peregrinations with many landscapes and a diary, the manuscript of which is now in the Copenhagen Library. He was particularly impressed by the beauty of Italian architecture and the radiant luminosity of Italy's atmosphere, which he rendered with great breadth of style and feeling in his brown wash studies. In this respect, *View of the Port of Valletta in Malta*, executed in 1664, is one of his finest works, especially admired by P. J. Mariette, who bought it at the Huquier sale in 1772, two years before his death: "J'ai de ce peintre un dessein de l'entrée du port de Malte qu'il a fait sur le lieu et qui porte cette date. On peut juger sur ce seul morceau de son habilité dans ce genre d'ouvrage; on n'y peut mettre plus de vérité ni plus d'intelligence; je n'ai rien vu qui en approche" (*Abecedario*, V, p. 196). The same site figures in four compositions in the Albertina; other attestations to Schellink's stay in Malta in 1664 are to be found in the *Atlas Blaeu* in the Vienna Nationalbibliothek.   R. B.

Jacob van Ruisdael

About 1628 - 1682

96. *View of Haarlem*

TECHNIQUE. Black chalk and gray wash. (16.4 x 23.9 cm.). Inscribed in lead pencil on the verso: *Buyten Haarlem* (near Haarlem).

PROVENANCE. Entered the Louvre before 1827. Inventory 23.017.

BIBLIOGRAPHY. J. Rosenberg, *Jacob van Ruisdael*, Berlin, 1928, no. 60, p. 114. Lugt, *Hollandais*, vol. II, 1931, no. 670, pl. XXX. *Les plus beaux Dessins du Louvre*, Exhibition Catalogue, Paris, Louvre, 1962, no. 56.

A student of his father, Isaack, and probably also of his uncle, Salomon, who then dominated the Haarlem group, Jacob van Ruisdael was to profoundly modify the concept of the Dutch landscape in the second half of the XVII century; he replaced the realism and objectivity of preceding works with an intense subjectivity, transposing observable reality in conformance with the demands of his forceful romantic genius. In 1656, after traveling to eastern Holland and to Germany, Ruisdael settled in Amsterdam, before returning, at the end of his life, to his native town of Haarlem, to which he had remained nostalgically attached. The Louvre drawing shows the dunes south of Haarlem; the expressive shading in black chalk and the touches of wash render the gray harmony of the melancholy landscape and the immensity of the sky streaked with clouds, throwing light and shadow on the vast expanse stretching towards the town in the distance. The same subject, seen slightly more from the right, reappears in a drawing in the same technique in the Kupferstichkabinett in Berlin (repr. W. Bernt, *Die Niederländischen Zeichner des 17. Jahrhunderts*, Munich, 1958, no. 507). R. B.

Cornelis Visscher

About 1629 - 1662

97. *Portrait of a Lady*

TECHNIQUE. Black chalk, with a few touches of gray wash, on vellum. (32.3 x 23.3 cm.). Signed in black chalk at the left: *C. Visscher fecit.*

PROVENANCE. Acquired by the Louvre during the Revolution. Inventory 23.117.

BIBLIOGRAPHY. Lugt, *Hollandais*, vol. II, 1931, no. 869, pl. LXXIII.
Portraits de femmes, Exhibition Catalogue, Paris, Orangerie, 1935, no. 171.
De Jérôme Bosch à Rembrandt, Exhibition Catalogue, Brussels, 1937, no. 156, pl. XCIV.
W. Bernt, *Die Niederländischen Zeichner des 17. Jahrhunderts*, Munich, 1958, no. 648, repr.

During his short life, Cornelis Visscher, brother of the engravers Jan and Lambert Visscher, became known for his burin engravings and above all for his admirable black chalk portraits, generally on vellum, thanks to which he ranks among the greatest portraitists of the XVII century. His penetrating psychology and sober execution relate him to Nanteuil in France. In the handsome drawing reproduced, the architectural decor and motif of the drapery are somewhat conventional, but the expressive intensity of the bright-eyed emaciated face, the rendition of the austere garment under the white tucker and the beautiful detail of the hand holding a flower are the work of a first-class artist. The same keen objectivity characterizes other portraits of elderly women, such as the one in Windsor dated 1652 (L. van Puyvelde, *Dutch Drawings... at Windsor Castle*, London, 1944, no. 730, pl. 94) or the Louvre drawing which belonged to P. J. Mariette (Lugt, no. 870, pl. LXXIV). The fact that Visscher was quickly discovered and appreciated in France accounts for the large number of his sheets in the Louvre portfolios. This portrait, together with those of a minister, *Jan Merius*, and a painter, *Philips Wouwerman* (Lugt, nos. 865-866, pl. LXXII), are among his major works.

R. B.

Willem van de Velde the Younger

1633 - 1707

98. *Naval Battle between Four Large Warships and Two Galleys*

TECHNIQUE. Pen and brown ink, gray wash, over a sketch in lead pencil. (15.4 x 30 cm.). Signed in pen and ink at lower left with the initials: *W. V. V.*

PROVENANCE. Acquired by the Louvre during the Revolution. Inventory 23.071.

BIBLIOGRAPHY. E. Michel, *Les Van de Velde*, Paris, n.d., repr. p. 52.
Lugt, *Hollandais*, vol. II, 1931, no. 816, pl. LXI.
Duquesne et la marine de son temps, Exhibition Catalogue, Dieppe, 1960, no. 40.

Like his father and master, Willem van de Velde (about 1611-1693), Van de Velde the Younger devoted himself to painting seascapes. Both artists took part in the important naval events of their time, accompanying the State fleet as observers. In 1673, they entered the service of King Charles II of England; the Louvre claims drawings by Van de Velde the Elder, executed at the marriage of William III of Orange and Mary Stuart, which depict the royal embarkation on the Thames (Lugt, nos. 806-807). Further trained by the painter, Simon de Vlieger, Van de Velde the Younger eventually surpassed his father in the rendition of atmosphere and variations of light; he emerged as the "prince" of XVII century Dutch seascape painters, leaving almost two thousand drawings, most of which are signed with his initials, often accompanied by the reference *J* ("Jonge," the Younger). Remarkable in the Louvre drawing are the intelligent indications in pen and ink which differentiate each embattled ship and the fluid, supple touches of gray wash that give life to the composition. Esaias van de Velde, Willem's uncle, and Adriaan van de Velde, his brother, were both painters and draughtsmen of considerable note (K. Z. van Manteuffel, *Die Künstler familie van de Velde*, Bielefeld, 1927).   R. B.

Gaspar van Wittel

About 1652 - 1736

99. *View of the Coliseum in Rome*

TECHNIQUE. Pen and brown ink, brown and gray wash, heightened with watercolor over a sketch in black chalk. (29.7 x 40.1 cm.). A strip of paper has been added by the artist at the lower part.

PROVENANCE. P. J. Mariette; stamp at lower left (Lugt 1852) and mounted with *GASPARDI VAN WITEL* inscribed in a cartouche; sale, Paris, 1775, part of lot no. 1068. Bought at this sale for the Royal Collection. Inventory 23.123.

BIBLIOGRAPHY. Lugt, *Hollandais*, vol. II, 1931, no. 923, pl. LXXXIV.
C. Lorenzetti, *Gaspare Vanvitelli*, Milan, 1934, p. 44.
W. Bernt, *Die Niederländischen Zeichner des 17. Jahrhunderts*, Munich, 1958, no. 694, repr.
G. Briganti, *Gaspar van Wittel e l'origine della vedutta settecentesca*, Rome, 1966, p. 309, repr. no. 165d.
Le Cabinet d'un grand amateur, *P. J. Mariette*, Exhibition Catalogue, Paris, Louvre, 1967, no. 209.

The view from the south side of the Coliseum extends through the arches to the church of S. Gregorio and the belfry of SS. Giovanni e Paolo at the left and the ruins of the Palatine Hill at the right. The interior of the Coliseum, treated by Van Wittel several times after his arrival in Rome, towards 1674, often inspired Northern artists working in the Eternal City, hence, for example, the views drawn by Nicolas Berchem, J. A. Bauer (repr. H. Egger, *Römische Veduten*, Vienna, 1931, vol. II, pls. 36-37) or W. Romeyn, (repr. Briganti, p. 23). Van Wittel's paricular sensitivity finds expression here in the especially felicitous composition, the free treatment in pen and ink of the foreground and the freshness of his watercolor notations. The present work and another watercolor, *Landscape with a Temple* (Inventory 23.122; Lugt, pl. LXXXIV), were bought for the Royal Collection at the Mariette sale in 1775. The collector's predilection for works executed by artists living in Rome like B. Breenbergh, Th. Wyck and Van Wittel reflects the taste of the period and is rewarded by the quality of the sheets presented here; Mariette acknowledged Van Wittel as: "Un des meilleurs peintres de vues qui ayent encore paru... Il est d'une justesse et il entre dans des détails qui causent une véritable admiration" (*Abecedario*, VI, p. 22).   R. B.

Jan van Huysum

1682 - 1749

100. *Vase of Flowers*

TECHNIQUE. Black chalk and watercolor on beige paper. (47.5 x 35.6 cm.).

PROVENANCE. The Royal Collection.
Inventory 22.669.

BIBLIOGRAPHY. Lugt, *Hollandais*, vol. I, 1929, no. 370, pl. LXV.
Intimistes Hollandais, Exhibition Catalogue, Paris, Louvre, 1953, no. 29.
W. Bernt, *Die Niederländischen Zeichner des 17. Jahrhunderts*, Munich, 1958, no. 317, repr.
J. G. van Gelder, *Prenten en Tekeningen*, Amsterdam, 1958, pl. 146.
C. White, *The Flower Drawings of Jan van Huysum*, Leigh-on-Sea, 1964, no. 109, p. 20, pl. 50.

In 1964, C. White catalogued this large format watercolor, which has preserved the brilliancy of its colored highlights, as a study for the painting in Sir Brian Mountain's collection (M. H. Grant, *Jan van Huysum*, Leigh-on-Sea, 1954, no. 11). The subject, a vase of flowers on a pedestal within the framework of a forest interior animated by statues with a bird's nest at the right, reappears in the painting in the Rijksmuseum dated 1735 (Grant, no. 1), studies for which are in the Berlin Kupferstichkabinett (White, nos. 4-5, pls. 3-4) and the Louvre (*idem*, no. 103, pl. 46); a watercolor, dated 1737, in the Pierpont Morgan Library in New York is directly related to the work reproduced (*idem*, no. 91, repr. pl. 37). Eldest son and student of the painter Justus van Huysum, Jan van Huysum's life was spent in Amsterdam devoted to the painting of flowers. The most brilliant artist in this field in XVIII century Holland, his work was sought by such famous collectors as the Duke d'Orléans, the King of Poland, the Prince of Hesse, the Elector of Saxony, the Duke of Mecklenbourg and Sir Robert Walpole. Not only was he admired for his skill as a painter and watercolorist, but also for the botanical exactitude of his floral representations. A large series of sketches of plants in the British Museum (White, nos. 22-84) are proof of the strict care given to the studies which served as a basis for the artist's exceptionally decorative and precise floral compositions.   R. B.

Inventory	Plate	Inventory	Plate	Inventory	Plate
18.498	28	20.148	38	22.919	86
18.579	4	20.154	39	22.970	80
18.582	5	20.170	48	23.002	94
18.588	19	20.183	56	23.024	95
18.590	13	20.185	50	23.017	96
18.597	9	20.187	52	23.071	98
18.602	7	20.195	59	23.117	97
18.608	8	20.196	57	23.123	99
18.658	30	20.212	54	RF 647	92
18.694	27	20.218	53	RF 664	93
18.696	25	20.224	55	RF 681	90
18.697	23	20.451	60	RF 700	58
18.727	29	20.474	46	RF 702	51
18.738	33	20.494	41	RF 738	3
18.741	32	20.592	43	RF 739	69
18.766	31	20.644	34	RF 841	76
18.804	40	20.649	36	RF 1079	12
18.838	1	20.721	74	RF 3812	35
18.865	21	20.737	24	RF 4113	10
18.867	17	20.871	68	RF 4651	26
18.898	2	20.900	75	RF 4652	16
18.919	18	22.213	72	RF 4663	78
18.936	20	22.394	89	RF 4688	79
18.944	22	22.545	77	RF 4918	66
19.592	71	22.579	91	RF 5168	15
19.728	42	22.598	73	RF 5639	11
19.779	49	22.669	100	RF 5640	6
19.836	44	22.677 *verso*	70	RF 6947	67
19.853	47	22.881	81	RF 11.746	85
19.907	65	22.883	82	RF 12.209	62
19.909	64	22.885	83		
19.970	61	22.892	84		
20.015	63	22.896	87		
20.053	37	22.917	88		

Index of Former Owners and Benefactors

I - INVENTORIES

1907-1938   INVENTAIRE GÉNÉRAL DES DESSINS DU MUSÉE DU LOUVRE ET DU MUSÉE DE VERSAILLES. ECOLE FRANÇAISE. Paris.
I, 1907 (2nd ed., 1933); II, 1908; III, 1909; IV, 1909; V, 1910; VI, 1911; VII, 1912; VIII, 1913; IX, 1921, by J. Guiffrey and P. Marcel. X, 1928, by J. Guiffrey, P. Marcel and G. Rouchès. XI, 1938, by G. Rouchès and R. Huyghe.

1929-1933   MUSÉE DU LOUVRE. INVENTAIRE GÉNÉRAL DES DESSINS DES ECOLES DU NORD. ECOLE HOLLANDAISE, by F. Lugt, Paris, I, 1929; II, 1931; III, 1933.

1937-1938   MUSÉE DU LOUVRE. INVENTAIRE GÉNÉRAL DES DESSINS DES ECOLES DU NORD. ECOLES ALLEMANDE ET SUISSE, by L. Demonts, Paris, I, 1937; II, 1938.

1949   MUSÉE DU LOUVRE. INVENTAIRE GÉNÉRAL DES DESSINS DES ECOLES DU NORD. ECOLE FLAMANDE, by F. Lugt, Paris, 1949, 2 vols.

II - PUBLICATIONS

1874   Vicount Both de Tauzia, MUSÉE NATIONAL DU LOUVRE. DON DE M. ET Mme PHILIPPE LENOIR, Paris, 1874 (miniatures nos. 208 to 281).

1882   V. Champier, LE MUSÉE DU LOUVRE. MODÈLES D'ART DÉCORATIF D'APRÈS LES DESSINS ORIGINAUX DES MAITRES ANCIENS, Paris, 1882.

        H. de Chennevières, LES DESSINS DU LOUVRE. I ECOLES FLAMANDE, HOLLANDAISE ET ALLEMANDE; II ECOLE ITALIENNE; III, 1 and 2, ECOLE FRANÇAISE, Paris, n.d. (1882).

1921   L. Demonts, MUSÉE DU LOUVRE. LES DESSINS DE MICHEL-ANGE, Paris, 1921.

1922   L. Demonts and Ch. Terrasse, Musée du Louvre. Catalogue de la donation Félix Doistau. Miniatures des XVIIIe et XIXe siècles, Paris, 1922.

L. Demonts, Musée du Louvre. Les dessins de Léonard de Vinci, Paris, n.d. (1922).

1923   L. Demonts, Musée du Louvre. Les dessins de Claude Gellée dit Le Lorrain, Paris, 1923.

1924   J. Guiffrey, Musée du Louvre. P.P. Prud'hon. Peintures, pastels et dessins, Paris, 1924.

1927   G. Rouchès, Musée du Louvre. Dessins italiens du XVIIe siècle, Paris, n.d. (1927).

1930   J. Bouchot-Saupique, Musée National du Louvre. Catalogue des pastels, Paris, 1930.

1936-1937   P. Jamot and J. Dupont, Les plus beaux dessins français du Musée du Louvre (1350-1900), Brussels, 1936-1937.

1938   G. Rouchès, Musée du Louvre. I. Quatorze dessins de Nicolas Poussin, Paris, 1938.

G. Rouchès, Musée du Louvre. II. Raphael. Quatorze dessins, Paris, 1938.

P. Lavallée, Musée du Louvre. III. J.H. Fragonard. Quatorze dessins, Paris, 1938.

P. Lavallée, Musée du Louvre. IV. Eugène Delacroix. Quatorze dessins, Paris, 1938.

1939   P. Lavallée, Musée du Louvre. V. Antoine Watteau. Quatorze dessins, Paris, 1939.

A. Blum, Musée du Louvre. VI. Rembrandt. Quatorze dessins, Paris, n.d. (1939).

J. Bouchot-Saupique, Musée du Louvre. VII. J.B. Greuze. Quatorze dessins, Paris, 1939.

M. Sérullaz, Musée du Louvre. VIII. Camille Corot. Quatorze dessins, Paris, 1939.

M. Sérullaz, Musée du Louvre. IX. J.L. David. Quatorze dessins, Paris, 1939.

G. Rouchès, Musée du Louvre. X. Andrea del Sarto. Quatorze dessins, Paris, 1939.

G. Rouchès, Musée du Louvre. XI. Maitres espagnols du XVIIe siècle. Quatorze dessins, Paris, 1939.

P. Lavallée, Musée du Louvre. XII. J.B. Oudry. Quatorze dessins, Paris, 1939.

1942	P. Lavallée, MUSÉE DU LOUVRE. XIII. FRANÇOIS BOUCHER. QUATORZE DESSINS, Paris, 1942.

P. Lavallée, MUSÉE DU LOUVRE. XIII. FRANÇOIS BOUCHER. QUATORZE DESSINS, Paris, 1942.

G. Rouchès, MUSÉE DU LOUVRE. XIV. FRA BARTOLOMMEO. QUATORZE DESSINS, Paris, 1942.

J. Bouchot-Saupique, MUSÉE DU LOUVRE. XV. JACQUES CALLOT. QUATORZE DESSINS, Paris, 1942.

J. Wilhelm, MUSÉE DU LOUVRE. XVI. FRANÇOIS LE MOYNE. QUATORZE DESSINS, Paris, 1942.

J. Alazard, MUSÉE DU LOUVRE. XVII. J.D. INGRES. QUATORZE DESSINS, Paris, 1942.

1943   E. Dacier, MUSÉE DU LOUVRE. XVIII. LE LIVRE DE CROQUIS DE GABRIEL DE SAINT-AUBIN. Paris, 1943.

1949   G. Rouchès, MUSÉE DU LOUVRE. LES DESSINS DE RAPHAEL, Paris, n.d. (1949).

1952   M. Sérullaz, MUSÉE DU LOUVRE. LES DESSINS DE DELACROIX. DESSINS, AQUARELLES ET LAVIS, Paris, n.d. (1952).

1966   CABINET DES DESSINS DU MUSÉE DU LOUVRE. I. DESSINS DE L'ECOLE FRANÇAISE, Paris, 1966. Twenty facsimiles.

1967   CABINET DES DESSINS DU MUSÉE DU LOUVRE. II. DESSINS DE L'ECOLE ITALIENNE, Paris, 1967. Twenty facsimiles.

n.d.   H. Prudent, LES DESSINS D'ARCHITECTURE AU MUSÉE DU LOUVRE. ECOLE FRANÇAISE, Paris, n.d. (about 1880).

n.d.   H. Prudent, LES DESSINS D'ARCHITECTURE AU MUSÉE DU LOUVRE. ECOLE ITALIENNE, Paris, n.d. (about 1880).

III - EXHIBITIONS

1797   NOTICE DES DESSINS ORIGINAUX, CARTONS, GOUACHES, PASTELS, EMAUX ET MINIATURES DU MUSÉE CENTRAL DES ARTS, EXPOSÉS POUR LA PREMIÈRE FOIS DANS LA GALERIE D'APOLLON, LE 28 THERMIDOR DE L'AN V DE LA RÉPUBLIQUE FRANÇAISE, First part, Paris, year V (1797). 2nd and 3rd revised and enlarged editions, Paris, year VII (1798-1799).

1802   NOTICE DES DESSINS ORIGINAUX, ESQUISSES PEINTES, CARTONS, GOUACHES, PASTELS, EMAUX, MINIATURES ET VASES ÉTRUSQUES, EXPOSÉS AU MUSÉE CENTRAL DES ARTS, DANS LA GALERIE D'APOLLON, EN MESSIDOR DE L'AN X DE LA RÉPUBLIQUE FRANÇAISE, Second part, Paris, year X (1802).

1803-1804   NOTICE DES DESSINS ORIGINAUX, ESQUISSES PEINTES, CARTONS, GOUACHES, PASTELS, EMAUX, MINIATURES ET VASES ÉTRUSQUES,

EXPOSÉS AU MUSÉE NAPOLÉON, DANS LA GALERIE D'APOLLON, EN MESSIDOR DE L'AN X DE LA RÉPUBLIQUE FRANÇAISE, 2nd ed., Paris, year XII (1803-1804).

1811   NOTICE DES DESSINS, DES PEINTURES, DES BAS-RELIEFS ET DES BRONZES, EXPOSÉS AU MUSÉE NAPOLÉON, DANS LA GALERIE D'APOLLON, Paris, 1811. 2nd and 3rd eds., Paris, 1814 and 1815.

1817   NOTICE DES DESSINS, PEINTURES, EMAUX ET TERRES CUITES ÉMAILLÉES, EXPOSÉS AU MUSÉE ROYAL, DANS LA GALERIE D'APOLLON, Paris, 1817. 2nd, 3rd and 4th eds., Paris, 1818, 1819 and 1820.

1838   NOTICE DES DESSINS PLACÉS DANS LES GALERIES DU MUSÉE ROYAL DU LOUVRE, Paris, 1838. 2nd, 3rd and 4th eds., Paris, 1839, 1841 and 1845.

1866   NOTICE DES DESSINS, CARTONS, PASTELS, MINIATURES ET EMAUX, EXPOSÉS DANS LES SALLES DU 1er ÉTAGE AU MUSÉE IMPÉRIAL DU LOUVRE. PREMIÈRE PARTIE : ECOLES D'ITALIE, ECOLES ALLEMANDE, FLAMANDE ET HOLLANDAISE, by F. Reiset, Paris, 1866. Other eds., Paris, 1871, 1872, 1876, 1878, 1879 and 1887.

1869   NOTICE DES DESSINS, CARTONS, PASTELS, MINIATURES ET EMAUX, EXPOSÉS DANS LES SALLES DU 1er ET DU 2e ÉTAGES AU MUSÉE IMPÉRIAL DU LOUVRE. DEUXIÈME PARTIE : ECOLE FRANÇAISE, DESSINS INDIENS, EMAUX, by F. Reiset, Paris, 1869. Another ed., Paris, 1883.

1879   NOTICE SUPPLÉMENTAIRE DES DESSINS, CARTONS, PASTELS ET MINIATURES DES DIVERSES ECOLES, EXPOSÉS DEPUIS 1869 DANS LES SALLES DU 1er ÉTAGE AU MUSÉE NATIONAL DU LOUVRE, by vicount Both de Tauzia, Paris, 1879. Other eds., Paris, 1887 and n.d.

1881   NOTICE DES DESSINS DE LA COLLECTION HIS DE LA SALLE, EXPOSÉS AU LOUVRE, by vicount Both de Tauzia, Paris, 1881.

1888   MUSÉE NATIONAL DU LOUVRE. DESSINS, CARTONS, PASTELS ET MINIATURES DES DIVERSES ECOLES, EXPOSÉS DEPUIS 1879 DANS LES SALLES DU 1er ÉTAGE. DEUXIÈME NOTICE SUPPLÉMENTAIRE, by vicount Both de Tauzia, Paris, 1888.

1900   CATALOGUE SOMMAIRE DES DESSINS, CARTONS, PASTELS, MINIATURES ET EMAUX, EXPOSÉS DANS LES SALLES DU 1er ET DU 2e ÉTAGES, Paris, n.d. (1900).

1922   DESSINS DE LÉONARD DE VINCI, Paris, Louvre, 1922.

DESSINS DE MICHEL-ANGE, Paris, Louvre, 1922.

1923   DESSINS DE CLAUDE GELLÉE DIT LE LORRAIN, Paris, Louvre, 1923.

1927   DESSINS ITALIENS DU XVIIe SIÈCLE, Château de Maisons-Laffitte and the Louvre, May-November 1927.

1929	DESSINS FRANÇAIS DU MILIEU DU XVIIᵉ SIÈCLE, Château de Maisons-Laffitte, 1929.
1930-1931	ŒUVRES PROVENANT DES DONATIONS FAITES PAR LA PRINCESSE LOUIS DE CROY ET LOUIS DEVILLER, Paris, Orangerie, 1930-1931.
1931	DESSINS DE LE BRUN ET DE MIGNARD, Château de Maisons-Laffitte, 1931. DESSINS ITALIENS XIVᵉ, XVᵉ ET XVIᵉ SIÈCLES, Paris, Orangerie, 1931.
1933	DESSINS ET AQUARELLES DE PAYSAGISTES FRANÇAIS DU XIXᵉ siècle, Paris, Orangerie, 1933.
1934	HOMMAGE AU CORRÈGE (1489-1534), Paris, Orangerie, 1934.
1935	PORTRAITS ET FIGURES DE FEMMES. PASTELS ET DESSINS, Paris, Orangerie, 1935.
1936	L'AQUARELLE DE 1400 A 1900, Paris, Orangerie, 1936.
1951	DESSINS DE LA COLLECTION MOREAU-NÉLATON, Paris, Louvre, 1951.
1952	DESSINS FLAMANDS DU XVIIᵉ SIÈCLE, Paris, Louvre, 1952. DESSINS FLORENTINS DU TRECENTO ET DU QUATTROCENTO, Paris, Louvre, 1952. DESSINS DE L'ECOLE ALLEMANDE, DE STEPHAN LOCHNER A ELSHEIMER, Paris, Louvre, 1952. HOMMAGE A LÉONARD DE VINCI, Paris, Louvre, 1952.
1953	LA COLLECTION CARLE DREYFUS, Paris, Louvre, 1953. DESSINS D'INTIMISTES HOLLANDAIS, Paris, Louvre, 1953.
1954	DESSINS ET MINIATURES DU XVIIIᵉ SIÈCLE, Paris, Louvre, 1954. QUELQUES ASPECTS DE LA VIE A PARIS AU XIXᵉ SIÈCLE, Paris, Louvre, 1954. DONATIONS ET ACQUISITIONS DU CABINET DES DESSINS DE 1946 A 1954, Paris, Louvre, 1954.
1955	DESSINS DE JEUNESSE DE DELACROIX, Paris, Louvre, 1955. REMBRANDT ET SON ENTOURAGE, Paris, Louvre, 1955. DESSINS DE MAITRES FLORENTINS ET SIENNOIS DE LA PREMIÈRE MOITIÉ DU XVIᵉ SIÈCLE, Paris, Louvre, 1955.
1956	DONATION D. DAVID-WEILL AU MUSÉE DU LOUVRE, MINIATURES ET EMAUX, Paris, Louvre, 1956. PASTELS DU XIXᵉ SIÈCLE, Paris, Louvre, 1956.
1957	THÉODORE CHASSÉRIAU, Paris, Louvre, 1957.

L'Enfant dans le dessin du XVᵉ au XIXᵉ siècles, Paris, Louvre, 1957.

Enluminures et dessins français du XIIIᵉ au XVIᵉ siècles, Paris, Louvre, 1957.

1958   Portraits dans le dessin français du XVIIIᵉ siècle, Paris, Louvre, 1958.

Dessins florentins de la collection Filippo Baldinucci, Paris, Louvre, 1958.

Monuments et sites d'Italie vus par les dessinateurs français, de Callot a Degas, Paris, Louvre, 1958.

1959   Dessins de Pierre-Paul Rubens, Paris, Louvre, 1959.

Le théatre et la danse en France aux XVIIᵉ et XVIIIᵉ siècles, Paris, Louvre, 1959.

1960   Dessins romains du XVIIᵉ siècle. Artistes italiens contemporains de Poussin, Paris, Louvre, 1960.

François-Marius Granet, Paris, Louvre, 1960.

Dessins français du XVIIᵉ siècle. Artistes français contemporains de Poussin, Paris, Louvre, 1960.

Dessins de Jean-François Millet, Paris, Louvre, 1960.

1961   Dessins allemands de la fin du XVᵉ siècle a 1550, Paris, Louvre, 1961.

1962   Dessins de Carrache, Paris, Louvre, 1962.

Dessins de Corot, Paris, Louvre, 1962.

Les plus beaux dessins du Louvre et quelques pièces célèbres des collections de Paris, Paris, Louvre, 1962.

1963   Delacroix. Dessins, Paris, Louvre, 1963.

Pastels et Miniatures des XVIIᵉ et XVIIIᵉ siècles, Paris, Louvre, 1963.

1964   Dessins de sculpteurs, de Pajou a Rodin, Paris, Louvre, 1964.

Dessins de l'Ecole de Parme, Paris, Louvre, 1964.

Pastels et Miniatures des XVIIᵉ et XVIIIᵉ siècles, Paris, Louvre, 1964.

1965   Le Seizième Siècle Européen. Dessins du Louvre, Paris, Louvre, 1965.

Boudin. Aquarelles et pastels, Paris, Louvre, 1965.

Giorgio Vasari, dessinateur et collectionneur, Paris, Louvre, 1965.

1966   PASTELS ET MINIATURES DU XIXe SIÈCLE, Paris, Louvre, 1966.

1967   LE CABINET D'UN GRAND AMATEUR, P.J. MARIETTE, Paris, Louvre, 1967.

      DESSINS FRANÇAIS DU XVIIIe SIÈCLE. AMIS ET CONTEMPORAINS DE P.J. MARIETTE, Paris, Louvre, 1967.

1967-1968 LE DESSIN A NAPLES DU XVIe AU XVIIIe SIÈCLE, Paris, Louvre, 1967-1968.